THE CARNEGIE
LIBRARY OF
PITTSBURGH

SOCIAL SCIENCES DEPARTMENT

DEMCO

## THE GLOBAL HISTORY SERIES

Under the general editorship of Leften Stavrianos

This series aims to present history in global perspective, going beyond national or regional limitations, and dealing with overriding trends and forces. The various collections of original materials span the globe, range from prehistoric times to the present, and include anthropology, economics, political science, and religion, as well as history.

The editor of this volume, Harold E. Driver, obtained his Ph.D. in anthropology from the University of California in 1936. He has taught since 1949 at Indiana University, where he holds the rank of professor. He is currently also a member of the International Development Research Committee at Indiana University. Dr. Driver has published more than fifty articles and reviews on many aspects of Indian life and the following books: *Comparative Studies of North American Indians* (with William C. Massey), 1957; *Indians of North America,* 1961; and *Ethnography and Acculturation of the Chichimeca-Jonaz of Northeast Mexico* (with Wilhelmine Driver), 1963. He has done extensive field work in California and Mexico, and has made briefer observations of native life in ten nations of Africa.

THE AMERICAS
ON THE EVE OF DISCOVERY

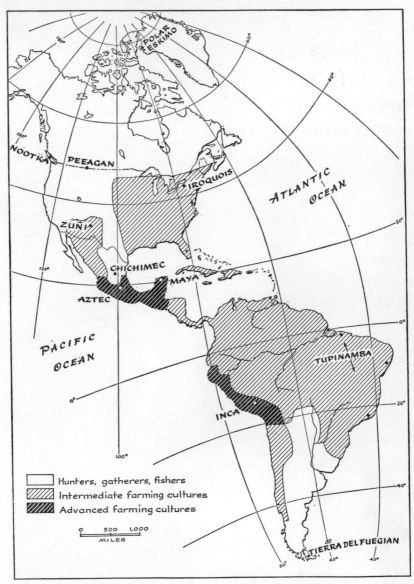

Major Types of Subsistence on the Eve of Discovery

# THE AMERICAS
# ON THE EVE OF DISCOVERY

EDITED BY HAROLD E. DRIVER

Prentice-Hall, Inc. / *Englewood Cliffs, N.J.*

A SPECTRUM BOOK

# PREFACE

The development of civilization in the Americas was almost totally independent of that in the Old World. The American Indians were isolated for millennia from the main hearths of ancient civilizations in the Old World. The achievements of the Aztecs and Mayas of Mexico and the Incas of Peru are, on the whole, somewhat less impressive than those of the Greeks and Romans, but they compare favorably with the earlier accomplishments of the second and third millennia B.C. in Egypt, Iraq, Pakistan, and China. The many parallels between the civilizations in the Americas and those of these four areas in the Old World demonstrate the inventive potential and genius of the human animal regardless of the color of his skin, the structure of his language, or the cultural poverty of his ancestors. Although the American Indians do not form a separate, organized faction in the economic and political affairs of the twentieth-century world, knowledge of their history and achievements is indispensable to a full understanding of global history and its implications.

The author wishes to thank the following persons and organizations for permission to quote the material which makes up the bulk of this anthology: Harper & Row, Publishers, Inc., for the use of Charles Darwin's *Journal of Researches into the Natural History and Geology of the Countries Visited during the Voyage of H.M.S. Beagle,* New York, 1846; the Research Center in Anthropology, Folklore, and Linguistics, Indiana University, for Harold and Wilhelmine Driver's *Ethnography and Acculturation of the Chichimeca-Jonaz of Northeast Mexico,* Bloomington, 1963; the Champlain Society of the University of Toronto for J. B. Tyrrell's *David Thompson's Narrative of his Explorations in Western America,* 1916; the Bureau of American Ethnology for Alfred Métraux's "The Tupinamba" in Bulletin 143, Vol. III, 1948, and Ruth Bunzel's "Introduction to Zuñi Ceremonialism" in Annual Report 47, 1932; Anthony F. C. Wallace and the *American Anthropologist* for "Dreams and Wishes of the Soul: A Type of Psychoanalytic Theory among the Seventeenth Century Iroquois," 1958; the Council of the Hakluyt Society of London for Clements R. Markham's translation of Cieza de León's *The Second Part of the Chronicle of Peru,* 1883; Ralph L. Roys and the Carnegie Institution of Washington for *The Indian Background of Colonial Yucatán,* Publication 548, 1943.

H.E.D.

# CONTENTS

## INTRODUCTION

# III / ADVANCED FARMING CULTURES

# CONCLUSION

# THE AMERICAS
# ON THE EVE OF DISCOVERY

# INTRODUCTION

## THE AMERICAN INDIANS: AN OVERVIEW

America was discovered a number of times before Columbus's dramatic voyage in A.D. 1492. The ancestors of the Indians probably first peopled the Americas some 20,000 years ago or more by way of a land bridge across what is now Bering Strait. At a much later date, after ocean-going boats had been invented, a few immigrants occasionally arrived from across the South Pacific or the North Atlantic. The best documented of these crossings are those of the Norsemen who negotiated the North Atlantic only a few centuries before Columbus made his famous voyage. None of these pre-Columbian contacts had any significant effect on the cultures of Europe. The voyage of Columbus, in contrast, attracted the attention of all Europe and initiated the most dramatic and far-reaching cross-fertilization of cultures in the history of the world. Within a half century after A.D. 1492 the Spanish had conquered the most advanced Indians in the Americas—those of Mexico and Peru—and had already begun to consolidate half the New World into a colonial empire. Exploration and colonization of Oceania and Australia came later, on the whole, and that of Africa very much later.

None of the Indians except the Mayas, Aztecs, and their neighbors had a system of writing, and the glyphs they used have not yet been satisfactorily deciphered. Although archeology has uncovered millions of material objects made and used by Indians before A.D.

1

1492, it is impossible to obtain full descriptions of Indian behavior before Europeans arrived and began to write the documents from which we now derive most of our information. However, by selecting the earliest known and most authentic accounts of Europeans we obtain pictures that differ little from the cultures of the Indians before their disturbance by Whites.

Seven of the selections quoted in this volume were written by eyewitnesses who were among the first to contact Indians in the New World. The other four were written by twentieth-century scholars most familiar with the earliest obtainable sources.

The word *Indian* was first used by Christopher Columbus to label the natives he encountered in the West Indies, because he thought he had reached the East Indies. The term was later extended to include all the native peoples of both North and South America from the Arctic to Tierra del Fuego. The variation in physical type, language, and culture over the 135 degrees of latitude inhabited by natives in the Americas is very great indeed, and is obscured by the use of the blanket term *Indian* for this conglomerate collection of peoples.

With respect to language, anthropological linguists have listed and classified about two thousand distinct Indian languages. This is almost as much variation in speech as has been found in the entire Old World, where about three thousand languages are known to have existed in A.D. 1500. Indian languages are not all equally different from each other but, like Old World languages, fall into language families. There has been little agreement among scholars on the number of Indian language families in the Americas but the figure would probably run to fewer than the number in the entire Old World.

The anthropologists' concept of culture, defined here as "all non-linguistic behavior," is not as objective as that of language and no one has ever counted cultures. However, in most cases where peoples speak distinct languages their cultures also show significant differences. Therefore there were about as many different cultures as there were languages in the New World in A.D. 1492. The cultures of the Indians have been grouped by leading books into about twenty-two culture areas; in the Old World the number of culture areas is somewhat greater. Culture areas and language families do not often coincide because language and culture can vary independently of each other and frequently, but not always, do so.

It is with respect to physical type that Indians show the most uniformity. The ancestors of 99 per cent of the Indians migrated to the Americas from Asia by way of Bering Strait and Alaska. Because there were no previous inhabitants with whom to mix, and the time, twenty thousand years or so, was too short for climatic or other environmental factors to produce marked changes in physique, Indians from Alaska to Tierra del Fuego are all grouped into the American Indian subdivision of the Asian (Mongoloid) major race. This does not mean that there are no significant biological differences from one Indian tribe to another, however. The most finespun classification of man's physique for the entire world gives about eighty varieties of man, and about 10 per cent of these are Indians. In short, the variation in Indian physique is only about 10 per cent of that in the entire world, whereas in numbers of languages it comes to about 40 per cent.

With such a tremendous variety of Indians to deal with in a volume of this length, it seemed best to select descriptions of specific tribes or nations rather than to become involved with a series of comparative generalizations. The eleven peoples described in the readings have been grouped into three classes according to the way they obtained their food: (1) hunting, gathering and fishing cultures; (2) intermediate farming cultures; (3) advanced farming cultures. This simple scheme is free of esthetic, moral, or other value judgments and makes no claim to being an evolutionary sequence into which all aspects of culture can be neatly pigeonholed. For instance, cannibalism is found in all three classes, although the details surrounding it differ greatly from one people or class to another. Slavery also occurs among all three kinds of food producers, and the most inhumane treatment of slaves in the history of the world was meted out by European masters in the sixteenth, seventeenth, and eighteenth centuries. Europe's leadership in science and technology in these centuries did not guarantee a parallel advancement in its concept of human rights as we view them today.

The Aztecs, Mayas, and Incas were chosen because their civilizations exemplify the most complex cultural achievement of the

Indians. They subsisted almost entirely on domesticated plants, which were intensively cultivated with the aid of irrigation and, less frequently, with fertilizers. The Aztecs and Mayas are the best-known and most distinguished pre-Columbian peoples in the culture area now called Meso-America (middle America), which includes the southern half of Mexico, south of the 22nd parallel of latitude, plus Guatemala. The Incas at the time of the Spanish conquest ruled all of the Central Andean culture area, which includes all the coastal and highland regions of present-day Peru and Bolivia, but not the tropical lowlands east of the Andes. At its maximum extension the Inca Empire also included the northern half of Chile, but this area never matched that of the Central Andes in general cultural development and is classified as a part of the Southern Andean culture area.

The intermediate farming cultures in South America are represented by the Tupinamba of Brazil, who occupied a small part of the huge Tropical Forest culture area. Domesticated plants cultivated by women provided the staple foods, but hunting and fishing were not neglected by the men. The same can be said of the Iroquois of New York State, who were chosen to represent the entire Eastern United States from about the 100th meridian (longitude) to the Atlantic Ocean. The Zuñi, although placed at the same general level as the Tupinamba and the Iroquois, differed in two respects: the men did the farming and they farmed more intensively, relying much less on hunting. The Zuñi represent the Indians of what is now Arizona and New Mexico.

The hunting, gathering, and fishing cultures did not farm at all and were entirely dependent on the wild animals, plants, and fish provided by nature. The Tierra del Fuegians belong in the Marginal (nonfarming) culture area of South America; the Chichimecs are characteristic of the little-known Northeast Mexican area; the Eskimos represent the Arctic; the Peeagans, the Plains area; and the Nootka, the Northwest Coast of North America. Although the Nootka lacked farming, as did the others in this group, the abundance of fish and sea mammals, which were most easily taken at favored localities, encouraged the establishment of permanent villages, a meticulous system of land tenure, a class structure with slaves at the bottom, and other social institutions more frequently found among farming peoples.

The selections have been chosen to illustrate *some* distinctive features of each society; there has been no attempt to present a comprehensive description of the society as a whole.

## 1 / THE IMPOVERISHED TIERRA DEL FUEGIANS OF CHILE AND ARGENTINA

*Tierra del Fuego, land of fire, was so named because of the signal fires used by the Indians to announce the presence of European ships. Although all vessels negotiating both the Atlantic and Pacific Oceans went around the Horn, through the Strait of Magellan, or through Beagle Channel, before the completion of the Panama Canal in 1914, they made only brief stops and had little contact with the natives until the nineteenth century. As will be apparent from Darwin's eyewitness report, the natives changed little in the period from Magellan (1520) to Darwin (1832-33). The Tierra del Fuegians are the southernmost inhabitants of the earth. In contrast to the Eskimos they had only the crudest clothing and housing, but were able to survive because the average daily temperature in winter did not go below 32° Fahrenheit. They would have died in the much colder climate of the Arctic without more adequate shelter. The cannibalism mentioned by Darwin is denied by a later investigator, a missionary named Thomas Bridges, who arrived at Beagle Channel in 1863 and lived for many decades with the natives. It is possible that both Darwin and Bridges are right: that cannibalism either was practiced at one locality and not at another or was coincident with Darwin's visit and not with that of Bridges. The Fuegians compete with the Chichimecs of Mexico for the lowest position on the totem pole of cultural achievement.*

Charles Darwin, *Journal of Researches into the Natural History and Geology of the Countries Visited during the Voyage of H.M.S. Beagle* (New York, 1846), I, 265-67, 272-77, 280-87, 290-92, 294-95.

I have not as yet noticed [mentioned] the Fuegians whom we had on board. During the former voyage of the Adventure and Beagle in 1826 to 1830, Captain Fitz Roy seized on a party of natives as hostages for the loss of a boat, which had been stolen, to the great jeopardy of a party employed on the survey; and some of these natives, as well as a child whom he bought for a pearl button, he took with him to England, determining to educate them and instruct them in religion at his own expense. To settle these natives in their own country was one chief inducement to Captain Fitz Roy to undertake our present voyage; and before the Admiralty had resolved to send out this expedition, Captain Fitz Roy had generously chartered a vessel, and would himself have taken them back. The natives were accompanied by a missionary, R. Matthews, of whom and of the natives Captain Fitz Roy has published a full and excellent account. Two men, one of whom died in England of smallpox, a boy and a little girl, were originally taken; and we had now on board, York Minster, Jemmy Button (whose name expresses his purchase-money), and Fuegia Basket. York Minster was a full-grown, short, thick, powerful man: his disposition was reserved, taciturn, morose, and when excited, violently passionate; his affections were very strong towards a few friends on board; his intellect good. Jemmy Button was a universal favourite, but likewise passionate; the expression of his face at once showed his nice disposition. He was merry, and often laughed, and was remarkably sympathetic with any one in pain: when the water was rough, I was often a little sea-sick, and he used to come to me and say, in a plaintive voice, "Poor, poor fellow!" but the notion, after his aquatic life, of a man being sea-sick, was too ludicrous, and he was generally obliged to turn on one side to hide a smile or laugh, and then he would repeat his "Poor, poor fellow!" He was of a patriotic disposition; and he liked to praise his own tribe and country, in which he truly said there were "plenty of trees," and he abused all the other tribes: he stoutly declared that there was no Devil in his land. Jemmy was short, thick, and fat, but vain of his personal appearance; he used always to wear gloves; his hair was neatly cut, and he was distressed if his well-polished shoes were dirtied. He was fond of admiring himself in a looking-glass; and a merry-faced little Indian boy from the Rio Negro, whom we had for some months on board, soon perceived this, and used to mock him: Jemmy, who was always rather jealous of the attention paid to this little boy, did not at all like this, and used to say, with rather a contemptuous twist of his head, "Too much skylark." It seems yet wonderful to me, when I think over all his many good qualities, that he should have been of the same race, and doubtless partaken of the same character, with the miserable, degraded savages whom we first met here. Lastly, Fuegia Basket was a nice, modest, reserved young girl, with a rather pleasing but sometimes sullen expression, and very quick in learning anything, especially languages. This she showed in picking up some Portuguese and Spanish when left on shore for only a short time at Rio de Janeiro and Monte Video, and in her knowledge of English. York Minster was very jealous of any attention paid to her; for it was clear he determined to marry her as soon as they were settled on shore. . . .

Great black clouds were rolling across the heavens, and squalls of rain, with hail, swept by us with such extreme violence, that the captain determined to run into Wigwam Cove. This is a snug little harbour, not far from Cape Horn; and here, at Christmas-eve, we anchored in smooth water. . . .

The cove takes its name of "Wigwam" from some of the Fuegian habitations; but every bay in the neighbourhood might be so called with equal propriety. The inhabitants, living chiefly upon shell-fish, are obliged constantly to change their place of residence; but they return at intervals to the same spots, as is evident from the piles of old shells, which must often amount to many tons in weight. . . .

The Fuegian wigwam resembles, in size and dimensions, a hay-cock. It merely consists of a few broken branches stuck in the ground, and very imperfectly thatched on one side with a few tufts of grass and rushes. The whole cannot be the work of an hour, and it is only used for a few days. At Goeree Roads I saw a place where one of these naked men had slept, which absolutely offered no more cover than the form of a hare. The man was evidently living by himself, and York Minster said he was "very bad man," and that probably he had stolen something. On the west coast, however, the wigwams are rather better, for they are covered with seal-skins. We were detained here several days by the bad weather. The climate is certainly wretched: the summer solstice was now passed, yet every day snow fell on the hills, and in the valleys there was rain, accompanied by sleet. The thermometer generally stood about 45°, but in the night fell to 38° or 40°. From the damp and boisterous state of the atmosphere, not cheered by a gleam of sunshine, one fancied the climate even worse than it really was.

While going one day on shore near Wollaston Island, we pulled alongside a canoe with six Fuegians. These were the most abject and miserable creatures I anywhere beheld. On the east coast the natives, as we have seen, have guanaco cloaks, and on the west they possess seal-skins. Amongst these central tribes the men generally have an otter-skin, or some small scrap about as large as a pocket-handkerchief, which is barely sufficient to cover their backs as low down as their loins. It is laced across the breast by strings, and, according as the wind blows, it is shifted from side to side. But these Fuegians in the canoe were quite naked, and even one full-grown woman was absolutely so. It was raining heavily, and the fresh water, together with the spray, trickled down her body. In another harbour, not far distant, a woman, who was suckling a recently-born child, came one day alongside the vessel, and remained there out of mere curiosity, whilst the sleet fell and thawed on her naked bosom, and on the skin of her naked baby! These poor wretches were stunted in their growth, their hideous faces bedaubed with white paint, their skins filthy and greasy, their hair entangled, their voices discordant, and their gestures violent. . . . At night, five or six human beings, naked, and scarcely protected from the wind and rain of this tempestuous climate, sleep on the wet ground coiled up like animals. Whenever it is low water, winter or summer, night or day, they must rise to pick shell-fish from the rocks; and the women either dive to collect sea-eggs, or sit patiently in their canoes, and with a baited hair-line, without any hook, jerk out little fish. If a seal is killed, or the floating carcass of a putrid whale discovered, it is a feast; and such miserable food is assisted by a few tasteless berries and fungi.

They often suffer from famine: I heard Mr. Low, a sealing-master, intimately acquainted with the natives of this country, give a curious account of the state of a party of one hundred and fifty natives on the west coast, who were very thin and in great distress. A succession of gales prevented the women from getting shell-fish on the rocks, and they could not go out in their canoes to catch seal. A small party of these men one morning set out, and the other Indians explained to him that they were going a four days' journey for food: on their return, Low went to meet them, and he found them excessively tired, each man carrying a great square piece of putrid whale's blubber, with a hole in the middle, through which they put their heads, like the Gauchos do through their ponchos or cloaks. As soon as the blubber was brought into a wigwam, an old man cut off thin slices, and muttering over them, broiled them for a minute, and distributed them to the famished party, who during this time preserved a profound silence. Mr. Low believes that whenever a whale is cast on shore, the natives bury large pieces of it in the sand, as a resource in time of famine; and a native boy, whom he had on board, once found a stock thus buried. The different tribes, when at war, are cannibals. From the concurrent, but quite independent evidence of the boy taken by Mr. Low, and of Jemmy Button, it is certainly true, that, when pressed in winter by hunger, they kill and devour their old women before they kill their dogs: the boy, being asked by Mr. Low why they did this, answered, "Doggies catch otters, old women no." This boy described the manner in which they are killed by being held over smoke and thus choked; he imitated their screams as a joke, and described the parts of their bodies which are considered best to eat. Horrid as such a death by the hands of their friends and relatives must be, the fears of the old women, when hunger begins to press, are more painful to think of; we were told that they then often run away into the mountains, but that they are pursued by the men, and brought back to the slaughter-house at their own firesides! . . .

The different tribes have no government or chief; yet each is surrounded by other hostile tribes, speaking different dialects, and separated from each other only by a deserted border of neutral territory: the cause of their warfare appears to be the means of subsistence. Their country is a broken mass of wild rocks, lofty hills, and useless forests; and these are viewed through mists and endless storms. The habitable land is reduced to the stones on the beach;

in search of food they are compelled unceasingly to wander from spot to spot, and so steep is the coast, that they can only move about in their wretched canoes. . . .

The Beagle anchored in Goeree Roads. Captain Fitz Roy having resolved to settle the Fuegians, according to their wishes, in Ponsonby Sound, four boats were equipped to carry them there through the Beagle Channel. . . .

The next day [January] (20th) we smoothly glided onwards in our little fleet, and came to a more inhabited district. Few, if any of these natives, could ever have seen a white man; certainly nothing could exceed their astonishment at the apparition of the four boats. Fires were lighted on every point (hence the name of Tierra del Fuego, or the land of fire), both to attract our attention, and to spread far and wide the news. Some of the men ran for miles along the shore. I shall never forget how wild and savage one group appeared: suddenly four or five men came to the edge of an overhanging cliff; they were absolutely naked, and their long hair streamed about their faces; they held rugged staffs in their hands, and, springing from the ground, they waved their arms round their heads, and sent forth the most hideous yells.

At dinner-time we landed among a party of Fuegians. At first they were not inclined to be friendly; for, until the captain pulled in ahead of the other boats, they kept their slings in their hands. We soon, however, delighted them by trifling presents, such as tying red tape round their heads. They liked our biscuit: but one of the savages touched with his finger some of the meat preserved in tin cases which I was eating, and feeling it soft and cold, showed as much disgust at it as I should have done at putrid blubber. Jemmy was thoroughly ashamed of his countrymen, and declared his own tribe were quite different, in which he was wofully mistaken. . . .

At night we endeavoured in vain to find an uninhabited cove, and at last were obliged to bivouac not far from a party of natives. They were very inoffensive as long as they were few in numbers, but in the morning (21st), being joined by others, they showed symptoms of hostility, and we thought that we should have come to a skirmish. A European labours under great disadvantages when treating with savages like these, who have not the least idea of the power of fire-arms. In the very act of levelling his musket he appears to the savage far inferior to a man armed with a bow and arrow, a spear, or even a sling. Nor is it easy to teach them our superiority except by striking a fatal blow. Like wild beasts, they do not appear to compare numbers; for each individual, if attacked, instead of retiring, will endeavour to dash your brains out with a stone, as certainly as a tiger under similar circumstances would tear you. Captain Fitz Roy, on one occasion, being very anxious, from good reasons, to frighten away a small party, first flourished a cutlass near them, at which they only laughed; he then twice fired his pistol close to a native. The man both times looked astounded, and carefully but quickly rubbed his head; he then stared a while, and gabbled to his companions, but he never seemed to think of running away. We can hardly put ourselves in the position of these savages, and understand their actions. In the case of this Fuegian, the possibility of such a sound as the report of a gun close to his ear could never have entered his mind. He perhaps, literally, did not for a second know whether it was a sound or a blow, and therefore very naturally rubbed his head. In a similar manner, when a savage sees a mark struck by a bullet, it may be some time before he is able at all to understand how it is effected; for the fact of a body being invisible from its velocity would, perhaps, be to him an idea totally inconceivable. Moreover, the extreme force of a bullet, that penetrates a hard substance without tearing it, may convince the savage that it has no force at all. Certainly I believe that many savages of the lowest grade, such as these of Tierra del Fuego, have seen objects struck, and even small animals killed by the musket, without being in the least aware how deadly an instrument it is.

22d.—After having passed an unmolested night, in what would appear to be neutral territory between Jemmy's tribe and the people whom we saw yesterday, we sailed pleasantly along. I do not know anything which shows more clearly the hostile state of the different tribes than these wide border or neutral tracts. Although Jemmy Button well knew the force of our party, he was at first unwilling to land amidst the hostile tribe nearest to his own. He often told us how the savage Oens men, "when the leaf red," crossed the mountains from the eastern coast of Tierra del Fuego, and made inroads on the natives of this part of the country. It was most curious to watch him when thus talking, and see his eyes gleaming and his whole face assume a new and wild expression. . . .

At night we slept close to the junction of Ponsonby Sound with the Beagle Channel. A small family of Fuegians, who were living in the cove, were quiet and inoffensive and soon joined our party round a blazing fire. We were well clothed, and though sitting close to the fire, were far from too warm; yet these naked savages, though further off, were observed, to our great surprise, to be streaming with perspiration at undergoing such a roasting. They seemed, however, very well pleased, and all joined in the chorus of the seamen's songs; but the manner in which they were invariably a little behindhand was quite ludicrous.

During the night the news had spread, and early in the morning (23d) a fresh party arrived, belonging to the Tekenika, or Jemmy's tribe. Several of them had run so fast that their noses were bleeding, and their mouths frothed from the rapidity with which they talked; and with their naked bodies all bedaubed with black, white, and red, they looked like so many demoniacs who had been fighting. We then proceeded (accompanied by twelve canoes, each holding four or five people) down Ponsonby Sound to the spot where poor Jemmy expected to find his mother and relatives. He had already heard that his father was dead; but as he had had a "dream in his head" to that effect, he did not seem to care much about it, and repeatedly comforted himself with the very natural reflection, "Me no help it." He was not able to learn any particulars regarding his father's death, as his relations would not speak about it.

Jemmy was now in a district well known to him, and guided the boats to a quiet, pretty cove named Woollya, surrounded by islets, every one of which and every point had its proper native name. We found here a family of Jemmy's tribe, but not his relations; we made friends with them, and in the evening they sent a canoe to inform Jemmy's mother and brothers. . . .

The next morning after our arrival (the 24th) the Fuegians began to pour in, and Jemmy's mother and brothers arrived. Jemmy recognised the stentorian voice of one of his brothers at a prodigious distance. The meeting was less interesting than that between a horse, turned out into a field, when he joins an old companion.

There was no demonstration of affection; they simply stared for a short time at each other, and the mother immediately went to look for her canoe. We heard, however, through York, that the mother had been inconsolable for the loss of Jemmy, and had searched everywhere for him, thinking that he might have been left after having been taken in the boat. The women took much notice of and were very kind to Fuegia. We had already perceived that Jemmy had almost forgotten his own language. I should think there was scarcely another human being with so small a stock of language, for his English was very imperfect. It was laughable, but almost pitiable, to hear him speak to his wild brother in English, and then ask him in Spanish ("no sabe?") whether he did not understand him.

Everything went on peaceably during the three next days, whilst the gardens were digging and wigwams building. We estimated the number of natives at about one hundred and twenty. The women worked hard, whilst the men lounged about all day long, watching us. They asked for everything they saw, and stole what they could. They were delighted at our dancing and singing, and were particularly interested at seeing us wash in a neighbouring brook; they did not pay much attention to anything else, not even to our boats. Of all things which York saw during his absence from his country, nothing seems more to have astonished him than an ostrich near Maldonado: breathless with astonishment, he came running to Mr. Bynoe, with whom he was out walking, "Oh, Mr. Bynoe, oh, bird all same horse!" Much as our white skins surprised the natives, by Mr. Low's account a negro cook to a sealing vessel did so more effectually; and the poor fellow was so mobbed and shouted at, that he would never go on shore again. Everything went on so quietly, that some of the officers and myself took long walks in the surrounding hills and woods. Suddenly, however, on the 27th, every woman and child disappeared. We were all uneasy at this, as neither York nor Jemmy could make out the cause. It was thought by some that they had been frightened by our cleaning and firing off our muskets on the previous evening; by others, that it was owing to offence taken by an old savage, who, when told to keep further off, had coolly spit in the sentry's face, and had then, by gestures acted over a sleeping Fuegian, plainly showed, as it was said, that he should like to cut up and eat our man. Captain Fitzroy [*sic*], to avoid the chance of an encounter, which would have been fatal to so many of the Fuegians, thought it advisable for us to sleep at a cove a few miles distant. Matthews, with his usual quiet fortitude (remarkable in a man apparently possessing little energy of character), determined to stay with the Fuegians, who evinced no alarm for themselves; and so we left them to pass their first awful night.

On our return in the morning (28th) we were delighted to find all quiet, and the men employed in their canoes spearing fish. . . .

February 6th.—We arrived at Woollya. Matthews gave so bad an account of the conduct of the Fuegians, that Captain Fitz Roy determined to take him back to the Beagle; and ultimately he was left at New Zealand, where his brother was a missionary. From the time of our leaving, a regular system of plunder commenced; fresh parties of the natives kept arriving: York and Jemmy lost many things, and Matthews almost everything which had not been concealed under ground. Every article seemed to have been torn up and divided by the natives. Matthews described the watch he was obliged always to keep as most harassing; night and day he was surrounded by the natives, who tried to tire him out by making an incessant noise close to his head. One day an old man, whom Matthews asked to leave his wigwam, immediately returned with a large stone in his hand: another day a whole party came armed with stones and stakes, and some of the younger men and Jemmy's brother were crying: Matthews met them with presents. Another party showed by signs that they wished to strip him naked and pluck all the hairs out of his face and body. I think we arrived just in time to save his life. Jemmy's relatives had been so vain and foolish, that they had showed to strangers their plunder, and their manner of obtaining it. It was quite melancholy leaving the three Fuegians with their savage countrymen; but it was a great comfort that they had no personal fears. York, being a powerful, resolute man, was pretty sure to get on well, together with his wife Fuegia. Poor Jemmy looked rather disconsolate, and would then, I have little doubt, have been glad to have returned with us. His own brother had stolen many things from him; and as he remarked, "what fashion call that?" he abused his countrymen, "all bad men, no sabe (know) nothing," and, though I never heard him swear before, "d——d fools." Our three Fuegians, though they had been only three years with civilized men, would, I am sure, have been glad to have retained their new habits; but this was obviously impossible. I fear it is more than doubtful whether their visit will have been of any use to them.

In the evening, with Matthews on board, we made sail back to the ship, not by the Beagle Channel, but by the southern coast. . . .

On the 5th of March we anchored in the cove at Woollya, but we saw not a soul there. We were alarmed at this, for the natives in Ponsonby Sound showed by gestures that there had been fighting; and we afterwards heard that the dreaded Oens men had made a descent. Soon a canoe, with a little flag flying, was seen approaching, with one of the men in it washing the paint off his face. This man was poor Jemmy, now a thin, haggard savage, with long, disordered hair, and naked, except a bit of a blanket round his waist. We did not recognise him till he was close to us; for he was ashamed of himself, and turned his back to the ship. We had left him plump, fat, clean, and well dressed; I never saw so complete and grievous a change. As soon, however, as he was clothed, and the first flurry was over, things wore a good appearance. He dined with Captain Fitz Roy, and ate his dinner as tidily as formerly. He told us he had "too much" (meaning enough) to eat, that he was not cold, that his relations were very good people, and that he did not wish to go back to England: in the evening we found out the cause of this great change in Jemmy's feelings, in the arrival of his young and nice-looking wife. With his usual good feeling, he brought two beautiful otter-skins for two of his best friends, and some spear-heads and arrows made with his own hands for the Captain. He said he had built a canoe for himself, and he boasted that he could talk a little of his own language! But it is a most singular fact, that he appears to have taught all his tribe some English: an old man spontaneously announced "Jemmy Button's wife." Jemmy had lost all his property. He told us that York Minster had built a large canoe, and with his wife Fuegia, had several months since gone to his own country, and had taken farewell by an act of consummate villany: he persuaded Jemmy and his mother to come with him, and then on the way deserted them by night, stealing every article of their property.

Jemmy went to sleep on shore, and in the morning returned, and remained on board till the ship got under weigh, which frightened his wife, who continued crying violently till he got into his canoe. He returned loaded with valuable property. Every soul on board was heartily sorry to shake hands with him for the last time. I do not now doubt that he will be as happy as, perhaps happier than, if he had never left his own country. Every one must sincerely hope that Captain Fitz Roy's noble hope may be fulfilled, of being rewarded for the many generous sacrifices which he made for these Fuegians by some shipwrecked sailor being protected by the descendants of Jemmy Button and his tribe! When Jemmy reached the shore, he lighted a signal fire, and the smoke curled up, bidding us a last and long farewell, as the ship stood on her course into the open sea.

# 2 / THE INTRANSIGENT CHICHIMECS OF MEXICO

*The Chichimecs were the nomadic bands that roamed over the northeastern third of Mexico, from one hundred miles north of Mexico City to Texas. They lived exclusively on wild animals, wild plants, and small quantities of fish provided by nature. They knew nothing of farming and had no domesticated animals, not even the dog. Their material possessions were as meager as those of the Tierra del Fuegians and their social and religious life was likewise simple. The report of Gonzalo de Las Casas, quoted below, refers to the Chichimecs living in what are now the Mexican states of Querétaro and Guanajuato. The culture of the Aztecs and their neighbors in the Valley of Mexico was one of the most advanced in the entire New World, yet at a distance of only one hundred airline miles to the north lived the impoverished Chichimecs. The reasons for this difference are complex and not obvious, but the reality of the difference is unassailable and provides one of the sharpest cultural contrasts anywhere in the world.*

*The Spanish fought the Chichimecs for more than two centuries, not decisively defeating them until 1748. The Chichimec wars cost the Spanish far more in blood, anguish and money than the short four-year campaign against the mighty Aztecs. The rank and file of Aztec citizens were so completely regimented that it never occurred to them to resist after their leaders had been captured or killed. The Chichimecs, in contrast, often fought to the last man to*

Harold E. Driver and Wilhelmine Driver, *Ethnography and Acculturation of the Chichimeca-Jonaz of Northeast Mexico, International Journal of American Linguistics*, XXIX, No. 2, Part II (1963), 15-18.

*preserve their freedom of action and, when captured, sometimes committed suicide rather than submit to the serfdom that the Spanish offered them.*

*The simple style of Las Casas is almost poetic at times and the translator, Wilhelmine Driver, has preserved the flavor of the original Spanish written in 1574.*

They have little or no interest in religion, no idols, no altars, no sacrifices, no prayer, no fasting, no letting of blood from tongue or ears. . . . The most they do is to make a few exclamations to the sky, while looking at some stars, in order to be safe from thunder and lightning. When they kill a captive they dance around him and also make the prisoner dance. . . . They are not horrified at the death of men, but kill them for pleasure and pastime, just as one kills a hare or deer.

They are extremely cruel and brutal. To a person they capture, whether man or woman, the first thing they do is to scalp him, leaving the entire crown bare, like the tonsure of a friar. I saw a Spaniard whom they had scalped, and also a Copuz woman who had lived without her scalp for many days and who, I believe, is still alive today. They also remove the sinews, which they use to tie the flints to their arrows. They take out the long bones of the arms and legs, while the victim is still alive, and also sometimes even the ribs, and perform a hundred other tortures until the victim finally dies. They wear, hanging at their backs, the scalps which they have taken, and some of these are from beautiful women with long blond locks; they also wear arm and leg bones as trophies. They show no mercy even to the corpses, on which they inflict every imaginable torture, hanging them from trees. They use them as targets, shooting arrows into their eyes, ears, tongue, and even genitals. A few days ago a captain whom I sent out found a corpse hanging from an oak tree, tortured in this manner and lacking one arm. . . . They fight nude, with bow and arrow, very skillfully and boldly; if they happen to be wearing clothes they undress for fighting. They always wear their quivers full of arrows, and carry four or five arrows in the bow hand to supply themselves more quickly. . . .

As I have said, they are cruel to the utmost in war, without regard for sex or age, killing and scalping both mother and child. . . . Although they take a few children and women as captives and make use of them, they never spare the life of a man. Their women seem to be more merciful, and have been known to give food to captives and weep over them, which the men never do.

They use no arms but the bow and arrow. With these they are so quick that one has been seen to shoot an arrow through both hands of a soldier holding an arquebus in his face, before the soldier could disarm him. . . . They shoot with such force that when they shot at the head of the horse of one soldier . . . the arrow passed through the horse's crownpiece, made of a double thickness of cowhide and a sheet of metal, and through the head and chest of the horse. . . . Many people have seen them perform such feats.

Their amusements are games, dancing, and drunkenness. Their most common game is played with a [rubber] ball which they call "batey," which is . . . heavy and made of a tree resin, very flexible and bouncy. They play it with the hips, dragging the buttocks on the ground, until one defeats the other. They also have games, known to all the Indians of these regions, with [mesquite] beans or arm and leg bones, and the prizes are arrows or sometimes hides. Another amusement is shooting at targets. Accompanied by their women, they shoot at a nopal leaf full of red juice, for augury when they are about to go to war.

Their dances are very different from those of the other peoples [in southern Mexico]. They dance at night, around the fire, linked arm in arm . . . in a way which seems confused, though there must be some order to it. . . . In the center of this dance they place the captive whom they intend to kill, and each one who enters the dance shoots an arrow into the victim. . . .

They have marriage, each having his own wife. Marriages are contracted through the mediation of the relatives. Through marriages enemies are often reconciled. Usually, when marrying into another band, the husband adopts the residence of his wife. They also have divorce, although usually it is the wife who repudiates the husband and not the reverse. All the work falls on the women, not only preparation of food but also carrying the children and all the loads on their backs when they move from place to place. The men carry nothing but their bow and arrows for fighting and hunting. The women serve the men like slaves, even giving them tunas [cactus pears] peeled. [The editors observed the latter in 1956.]

They bear their children with great distress, because, having no houses and roaming constantly, they often give birth while travelling. Even with the placenta hanging and dripping blood they walk on as if they were sheep or cows. They wash their infants, or, if there is no water, clean them with herbs. They have nothing to give their children but their own milk, nor do they wrap them in blankets, because they have none. They have no cradles, no houses for shelter, nothing more than a piece of cloth or a rock, and in such harsh conditions they live and rear their children.

Their food consists of fruit and wild roots. They neither sow nor gather any sort of vegetables, nor do they have any cultivated trees. The fruits which they use most are tunas, of many varieties and colors, some of them delicious. They also eat the fruit of another tree called mesquite, a well-known wild tree which bears pods like string beans, which they eat and from which they make bread to keep and eat when the fresh fruit is gone. They have another fruit which we call dates; although the trees which bear them are not date palms they resemble them. Of the roots which they eat, some resemble sweet potatoes or yuca. . . .

The maguey is a great help and support to them, for it is never lacking. They make use of all of it, as do the people of New Spain [southern Mexico], except that they do not make clothing from it. They eat the leaves and the root cooked in an earth oven which they call "mizcale," and it is good food, and they also make wine from it. All the roots mentioned above they also cook in the earth oven, since they are inedible raw.

They support themselves mostly on game, which they hunt every day. They shoot hares on the run, and deer and birds and other game, even rats. A few of them also fish. Some fish with arrows; others catch the fish in weirs or basket nets, and some swim and dive for fish. If they happen to kill a deer, the woman must come after it, because the man does not carry loads. The women also have to gather fruit and roots, and clean and cook them, after returning from the hunt. . . .

The Mexicans make [alcoholic] drinks only from maguey. The

Chichimecs have the same, and also others made of tunas and of mesquite. Thus they have three different kinds of wine, on which they get drunk very often. . . . They have no vessels of clay or wood, but only those which they make of fibre so tightly woven and compressed that they will hold water; some of these are as big as a large basket. Because of their experience of the harm which can come to them during a drunken spree, they have the custom that, while they are getting drunk, the women stay apart from them and hide their bows and arrows. They never all get drunk together, but always leave someone on guard, so that they will not be caught unaware and be captured or killed.

They go completely naked. The women wear a belt of deer skins, the others go entirely nude. Among themselves they are not ashamed to be naked and do not permit clothing. When they parley with us they show some modesty, and seek the wherewithal, if only rags and herbs, to cover their privy parts. They frequently paint themselves, smearing on red ocher and other minerals of black, yellow, and all colors.

For mourning they crop their hair and smudge themselves with black, and continue thus for some time. To remove this, they make a feast and invite their friends, and, in their company, go and bathe themselves. They do not bury their dead, but burn them and save the remains or ashes in small bags which they carry with them. The ashes of enemies they scatter to the winds. . . .

# 3 / THE ISOLATED POLAR ESKIMOS OF GREENLAND

*The Polar Eskimos, the northernmost people on the earth, had no contact whatsoever with Europeans until Captain John Ross of the British Royal Navy discovered them in 1818. But what is more remarkable is their complete isolation from other groups of Eskimos as well for a period estimated at about five hundred years. Numbering only a few hundred, this band of hardy Eskimos had lived with complete self-sufficiency apart from all other human beings for centuries, and regarded John Ross and his men as spirits from the sun or moon who might wish to kill them. There is no other instance in the historical or anthropological record of any people living in such extreme isolation. The rapidity with which the Eskimo men first encountered by Ross adjusted to their European visitors is amazing and illustrates the high order of intelligence and pragmatic adaptability of these natives. Ross calls them Arctic Highlanders, but the term Polar Eskimos is more often used by anthropologists today.*

About ten o'clock this day, we were rejoiced to see eight sledges, driven by the natives, advancing by a circuitous route towards the place where we lay: they halted about a mile from us, and the people alighting, ascended a small iceberg, as if to reconnoitre. After remaining apparently in consultation for nearly half an hour, four of them descended, and came towards the flag-staff, which, however, they did not venture to approach. In the mean time a

John Ross, *A Voyage of Discovery* (London, 1819), pp. 107-32, 136-38, 168-72, 176-87.

24

white flag was hoisted at the main in each ship, and John Sacheuse dispatched, bearing a small white flag, with some presents, that he might endeavour, if possible, to bring them to a parley. This was a service which he had most cheerfully volunteered, requesting leave to go unattended and unarmed, a request to which no objection could be made, as the place chosen for the meeting was within half a mile of the Isabella. It was equally advantageous to the natives, a canal, or small chasm in the ice, not passable without a plank, separating the parties from each other, and preventing any possibility of an attack from these people, unless by darts. . . .

Sacheuse, after a time, thought he could discover that they spoke the Humooke dialect, drawling out their words, however, to an unusual length. He immediately adopted that dialect, and, holding up the presents, called out to them, *Kahkeite,* "Come on!" to which they answered, *Naakrie, naakrieai-plaite,* "No, no—go away;" and other words which he made out to mean, that they hoped we were not come to destroy them. The boldest then approached to the edge of the canal, and drawing from his boot a knife, repeated, "Go away"; "I can kill you." Sacheuse, not intimidated, told them he was also a man and a friend, and, at the same time, threw across the canal some strings of beads and a chequed shirt; but these they beheld with great distrust and apprehension, still calling, "Go away, don't kill us." Sacheuse then threw them an English knife, saying, "Take that." On this they approached with caution, picked up the knife, then shouted and pulled their noses; these actions were imitated by Sacheuse, who in return, called out, *"Heigh, yaw!"* pulling his nose with the same gesture. They now pointed to the shirt, demanding what it was, and when told it was an article of clothing, asked of what skin it was made. Sacheuse replied, it was made of the hair of an animal which they had never seen; on which they picked it up with expressions of surprise. They now began to ask many questions; for, by this time, they found the language spoken by themselves and Sacheuse, had sufficient resemblance to enable them to hold some communication.

They first pointed to the ships, eagerly asking, "What great creatures those were?" "Do they come from the sun or the moon?" "Do they give us light by night or by day?" Sacheuse told them that he was a man, that he had a father and mother like themselves; and, pointing to the south, said that he came from a distant country in that direction. To this they answered, "That cannot be, there is nothing but ice there."

They again asked, "What creatures these were?" pointing to the ships; to which Sacheuse replied, that "they were houses made of wood." This they seemed still to discredit, answering, "No, they are alive, we have seen them move their wings." Sacheuse now enquired of them what they themselves were; to which they replied, they were men, and lived in that direction, pointing to the north; that there was much water there; and that they had come here to fish for sea-unicorns. It was then agreed, that he should pass the chasm to them, and he accordingly returned to the ship to make his report, and to ask for a plank.

During the whole of this conversation I had been employed, with a good telescope, in observing their motions; and beheld the first man approach with every mark of fear and distrust, looking frequently behind to the other two, and beckoning them to come on, as if for support. They occasionally retreated, then advanced again, with cautious steps, in the attitude of listening, generally keeping one hand down by their knees, in readiness to pull out a knife which they had in their boots; in the other hand they held their whips with the lash coiled up; their sledges remained at a little distance, and the fourth man being apparently stationed to keep them in readiness for escape. Sometimes they drew back the covering they had on their heads, as if wishing to catch the most distant sounds; at which time I could discern their features, displaying extreme terror and amazement, while every limb appeared to tremble as they moved. Sacheuse was directed to entice them to the ship, and two men were now sent with a plank, which was accordingly placed across the chasm. They appeared still much alarmed, and requested that he only should come over; he accordingly passed to the opposite side, on which they earnestly besought him not to touch them, as if he did, they should certainly die. After he had used many arguments to persuade them that he was flesh and blood, the native who had shown most courage, ventured to touch his hand; then pulling himself by the nose, set up a shout, in which he was joined by Sacheuse and the other three. The presents were then distributed, consisting of two or three articles of clothing, and a few strings of beads; after which Sacheuse exchanged a knife for one of theirs. . . .

Sacheuse now laboured to assure them, that the ship was only a wooden house, and pointed out the boat, which had been hauled on the ice to repair; explaining to them that it was a smaller one of the same kind. . . .

Their attention being again called to the boat, where the carpenter's hammer and nails still remained, they were shown the use of these articles, and no sooner were they aware of their purposes than they showed a desire to possess them, and were accordingly presented with some nails. They now accompanied us to that part of the bow from which a rope-ladder was suspended, and the mode of mounting it was shown them, but it was a considerable time ere we could prevail on them to ascend it: at length the senior of them, who always led the way, went up, and was followed by the rest. The new wonders that now surrounded them on every side caused fresh astonishment, which, after a moment's suspense, always terminated in loud and hearty laughter. The most frequent ejaculation of surprise was *Heigh, yaw!* and when particularly excited by any more remarkable object than the rest, they pronounced the first syllable of the interjection many times with peculiar rapidity and emphasis, extending wide their arms, and looking at each other at the end of the exclamation with open mouths, as if in breathless consternation.

Their knowledge of wood seemed to be limited to some heath of a dwarfish growth, with stems no thicker than the finger, and accordingly they knew not what to think of the timber they saw on board. Not being aware of its weight, some of them successively seized on the spare top-mast, evidently with the view of carrying it off; and as soon as they became familiar with the people around them, they showed that desire of possessing what they admired, which is so universal among savages. . . .

The three men remaining were now handed down to my cabin, and shown the use of the chairs, which they did not comprehend, appearing to have no notion of any other seat than the ground. . . . We showed them papers, books, drawings, and various mathematical instruments, which produced only the usual effect of astonishing them; but on being shown the prints in Cook's voyage of the natives of Otaheite, they attempted to grasp them, evidently comprehending that they were the representations of human beings. . . .

They were now conducted to the gunroom, and afterwards round the ship, but without appearing to distinguish any thing particularly, except the wood, in her construction, stamping on the deck, as if in surprise at the quantity of the valuable material. . . .

They were now loaded with various presents, consisting of some articles of clothing, biscuit, and pieces of wood, in addition to which the plank that had been used in crossing the chasm was given to them. They then departed, promising to return as soon as they had eaten and slept, as we had no means of explaining to them what to-morrow meant. The parting was attended with the ceremony of pulling noses on both sides.

After they had reached and crossed the chasm, they were observed by some men, who had been sent to accompany them, throwing away the biscuit, and splitting the plank, which was of teak, into small pieces, for the purpose of dividing it among the party. Soon after this they mounted their sledges, and drove off in a body, hallooing, apparently, in great glee. . . .

During this day we made some attempts to discover from Sacheuse what further particulars he had learned respecting the natives; the hurry of the preceding having prevented us from conversing so fully with him as we could have wished. Among other less important particulars, we found that they had sent their women and children to the mountains, and that their original intention of coming to the ships was, to request us to go away, and not to destroy them: they also informed him, that they had watched for some time, to see whether the ships would fly to the sun or the moon, from one of which they concluded we must have come. One of their companions had been so much alarmed, that he ran off to the mountains, and had not returned.

We also found, what he had forgotten to tell us before, that the iron was procured from a mountain near the shore. They had informed him that there was a rock of it, or more, (for it could not at this time be ascertained which,) and that the pieces from which the blades of their knives were made were cut off by means of a sharp stone. . . .

We had not remained long at our new moorings, before we were gratified by the appearance of three of the natives at a distance. . . . It being proposed that they should drive close to the ship on their sledges, the eldest got into his sledge, for this purpose, and we had thus an opportunity of witnessing the mode in which he managed his dogs. These were six in number, each having a collar of seal-skin, two inches wide, to which the one end of a thong, made of strong hide, about three yards long, was tied; the other end being fastened to the fore part of the sledge: thus they all stood nearly abreast, each drawing by a single trace, without reins. No sooner did they hear the crack of the whip, than they set off at full speed, while he seemed to manage them with the greatest ease, guiding them partly by his voice, and partly by the sound of the whip. On approaching our sailors, however, they became so terrified, that it was with some difficulty they could be stopped. . . .

The Origin of the Arctic Highlanders is a question as yet involved in peculiar obscurity. They exist in a corner of the world among the most secluded which has yet been discovered, and have no knowledge of any thing beyond the boundary of their own country: nor have they any tradition whence they came; appearing, until the moment of our arrival, to have believed themselves to be the only inhabitants of the universe, and to have considered all the rest of the world as a mass of ice. It is generally believed by the natives of South Greenland, that they are themselves descended from a nation in the north. . . . The similarity of the language proves that they are the same people; and it appears most probable, that South Greenland has been peopled from the north, and that the northern parts of Baffin's Bay have been, in the same manner, originally peopled from America. . . . It is not difficult to account for their having no canoes, as they labour under a total want of wood, and at any rate they could not use them above a few weeks; but it is, at the same time, not easy to understand how they should be ignorant, even traditionally, of the existence of a boat. They present a solitary instance, as far as we know, and apparently a very singular one, of a maritime and fishing tribe unacquainted with any means of floating on the water. The want of wood is scarcely an excuse for this ignorance, as a people accustomed to make sledges from bones and skins, could find no great difficulty in constructing some kind of boat of the same materials.

The Dress of the Arctic Highlanders consists of three pieces, which are all comprised under the general name of *"tunnick."* The upper one is made of seal-skin, with the hair outside, and is similar to the woman's jacket of the South Greenlander; being open near the top only, so as to equal the size of the wearer's face. At the bottom it is formed like a shirt, terminating in a tongue before and behind; the hood part being neatly trimmed with fox's skin, and made to fall back on the shoulders, or cover the head, as required. This is lined, in general, with eider-duck or awk-skins; and the lining, being close at the bottom and open near the breast, serves as a pocket. The next piece of dress, which scarcely reaches the knee, is also uncomfortably small in the upper part; so that, in stooping, the skin is exposed. This is made of bear's or dog's skin, and fastened with a string. The boots are made of seal-skin, with the hair inwards, the soles being covered with seahorse hide; they reach over the knees, and meet the middle part of the dress. The whole of these are made by the women; the needles used being of ivory, and the thread of the sinews of the seal: the seams are so neat that they can scarcely be distinguished. They informed us, that in the winter, or as the weather became colder, they had a garment of bear-skins, which they put on as a cloke, but this we did not see, nor were we able to persuade them to spare any part of their dress. . . .

Ervick, being the senior of the first party that came on board, was judged to be the most proper person to be questioned on the subject of religion. The word "angekok," which means a conjuror, or sorcerer, was then pronounced to him in the South Greenland language. He said, that they had many of these: that it was in their power to raise a storm, or make a calm, and to drive off seals, or to bring them: that they learned this art from old Angekoks, when young: that the people were afraid of them; but that they had generally one in every family. . . . Although we could thus obtain no proof that this people had any notions of a Supreme Being, or of a spirit, good or bad, the circumstance of their having conjurers, and the tale of their going to the moon after death, render it probable that they possess some religious ideas, however barbarous, and that the unsatisfactory information which we obtained on this head, arose chiefly from our ignorance of their language, and from the very imperfect and limited communication which we had with them. . . .

These [their] houses are built entirely of stones, the walls being sunk three feet into the earth, and raised to three feet above it; the roof is in the form of an arch, and such holes as would admit air are filled up with mud: they have no windows. The entrance is by a long, narrow, and nearly under-ground passage. The floor is covered with skins, on which they sit or sleep; several families living in one house, and each family having a lamp made of a hollowed stone, suspended from the roof, in which they burn the oil, or rather the blubber of the seal and sea-unicorn [narwhal], using dried moss for a wick: their fire is produced by friction, and, as we understood, from iron and stone. The lamp, which is never extinguished, serves for light and warmth, as well as for cooking; and we ascertained that they had methods both of boiling and of roasting, or scorching, their meat; occupations which fall entirely on the women. They eat all kinds of animal food; but the seal and sea-unicorn are preferred, as being more oily and agreeable to their palates. Dogs are also esteemed excellent food, and are bred as live stock, as well as for drawing the sledge; but they are only eaten in winter, when no other food can be obtained. The men catch the seals, either when they are asleep, or by lying down near the holes in the ice, making a peculiar noise, by which they are brought to the surface. When the animal appears they imitate his cry, or grunt, and by this means induce him to come on the ice and approach them; when within reach, they strike him on the nose with a spear made of sea-unicorn's horn, and soon despatch him.

The sea-unicorn is taken by a harpoon, the barbed part of which is about three inches long; having a line attached to it of about five fathoms in length, the other end of which is fastened to a buoy of a seal's skin, made into a bag and inflated. The blade is fixed on the end of the shaft in such a manner that it may be disengaged from the handle after it is fixed in the animal, and the shaft is then pulled back by a line, which is tied to it for the purpose. When struck, he immediately plunges, and carries down with him the seal-skin buoy, which fatigues him. As he must come up in some pool to respire, like the whale, he is followed and killed with spears; and as he frequents the chasms and pools in the ice, he falls an easy prey to the natives.

We could not learn the precise manner in which they kill the bears, but they informed us that they attacked them in the water. The foxes and hares are taken in traps, made of stones, resembling a small grotto, and having a narrow entrance, which is closed by a stone that falls down when the animals enter to take the bait left within it. The natives described to us an animal which they called *humminick,* but said it was too large for them to kill; it has, by their account, a horn on its back, and is very swift; I therefore supposed that it was the reindeer. . . . The dogs, which are the only animals that have been domesticated by the Arctic Highlanders, are of various colours, but chiefly of a dun hue; they are the size of a shepherd's dog, with a head like a wolf, and a tail like a fox; their bark resembles the latter, but they have also a howl like the former.

The Arctic Highlanders never hunt, nor travel to any distance, except on their sledges, and they always carry with them their spears and knives: from the rapidity with which they seem to drive, it may be fairly conjectured that they can travel fifty or sixty miles a day; distances, indeed, which are known to be performed by the natives of South Greenland. The habits of this people appear to be filthy in the extreme; their faces, hands, and bodies, are covered with oil and dirt, and they seem never to have been washed since they were born. Their hair was matted with filth, yet they seemed very tenacious of it; for, when a small piece was cut off from the head of one of Meigack's sons, both he and his father were much displeased, and showed great uneasiness until it was returned; when it was carefully wrapped in a piece of seal-skin, and put by the former into his pocket. We learned that each man took one wife, when he was able to maintain a family; if she had children, he took no other, nor was she permitted to have another husband; but if otherwise, the man may take another wife, and so on a third, until they have children; the women having the same privilege. Ervick spoke very affectionately of his wife, who he said was a good one, because she had six sons; when they took or begged any fanciful thing, such as a looking-glass or a picture, they all said it was for their wives.

They also showed much respect to their mothers: as one of them refused to part with his sledge, and another with his jacket, lest their mothers should be displeased. The dress of the women is, from what we could collect, the same as that of the men. We could not discover whether they lived to a great age or not, as the old people had been sent to the mountains, or concealed on our approach; nor did we see any of the children. I asked both Ervick and Meigack if they would spare one of their sons, which they refused to do; nor could either of them be tempted by any presents to overcome their objections. Indeed, none of them were willing to leave their country; they seemed perfectly happy and contented: their clothing was in good condition and very suitable to the climate, and by their own account, they had abundance of provisions. They all acknowledged Tulloowah as their king, and represented him as a strong man, very good, and very much beloved; the name of his residence was Petowack, and they described it as being near a large island, in the middle of their country, which could be no other than Wolstenholme Island. He had a large house built of stone, which they described to be nearly as large as the ship: they said that there were many houses near it, and that the mass of the natives lived there; that they paid him a portion of all they caught or found, and that they returned there when the sun went away, with the fruits of their labours. They could not be made to understand what was meant by war, nor had they any warlike weapons; I therefore gave strict and positive orders that no fire-arms, or other warlike weapons, should be shown them, or given to them on any account, and, when they were with us, all shooting-parties were called in. They seemed to have no peculiar diseases among them, nor did we see any deformed persons.

Such is the substance of what we collected in our short intercourse with this interesting people.

# 4 / THE PROUD PEEAGANS OF MONTANA AND ALBERTA

*The narrative quoted below was written by David Thompson when he was about seventy years old, but much of the detail had previously been written in notebooks between the years 1784 and 1807. It is unsurpassed for its description of eighteenth-century Plains Indian life. The autobiography of Saukamappee in the last half of this report by Thompson begins about 1730 and ends soon after the smallpox epidemic of 1781. In the beginning of this period the Peeagans had neither guns nor horses, but were entirely dependent on the bow and arrow for hunting and warfare and on their own legs for transportation. The ten guns mentioned in the battle around 1730 were possessed by the three Cree and the seven Assiniboin braves who had joined the war party of the Peeagans; the Peeagans themselves had none. The guns came from British trading posts farther east, probably from York Factory on Hudson Bay, and reached the Cree and Assiniboin first because these tribes were closer to the source of supply.*

*The horses of the Snake (Shoshoni) Indians, in contrast, had been relayed northward from the Spanish ranches in what is now New Mexico. The three northern Plains tribes mentioned in the autobiography all obtained their first horses from the west; the Peeagans directly from the Snakes, and the more eastern tribes from the Peeagans as well as from the Snakes.*

*Those Plains peoples who acquired either guns or horses had an advantage in hunting and warfare over those who had neither;*

J. B. Tyrrell, ed., *David Thompson's Narrative of his Explorations in Western America* (Toronto: The Champlain Society, 1916), pp. 328-38, 345-51, 353-55, 357.

*and those who had both had an edge on those with only one or the other. By the beginning of the nineteenth century all Plains tribes had both guns and horses, which, added to the demand for buffalo hides, brought about the virtual extermination of the buffalo by 1880. As the buffalo became scarcer, the competition for the remainder became keener and vastly increased the toll of Indian lives. The expansion of the United States westward after the Civil War succeeded in defeating the surviving Indians and in impounding them in reservations. Thus the horse and the gun, which were welcomed by the Indians, ultimately increased the rate at which they were overcome by Whites.*

*The common notion that the expressionless faces of Indians in public reflect their lack of normal human emotions is shown by Thompson to be wrong. Love was important to all young people, who frequently eloped to avoid the girl's being married off to an old man of her father's choice. The case of the young woman who asked the brothers of her deceased husband to kill her so that her soul could join that of her husband in the afterworld is as tragic as anything in European drama.*

The Peeagans, with the tribes of the Blood, and Blackfeet Indians, who all speak the same language, are the most powerful of the western and northern plains, and by right of conquest have their west boundary to the foot of the Rocky Mountains, southward to the north branches of the Missisourie [sic], eastward for about three hundred miles from the Mountains and northward to the upper part of the Saskatchewan. Other tribes of their allies also at times hunt on part of the above, and a great extent of the Plains, and these great Plains place them under different circumstances, and give them peculiar traits of character from those that hunt in the forests. These latter live a peaceable life, with hard labor, to procure provisions and clothing for their families, in summer they make use of canoes, and in winter haul on sleds all they have, in their frequent removals from place to place. On the other hand the Indians of the Plains make no use of canoes, frequently stay many days in a place, and when they remove have horses and dogs, both in summer and winter to carry their baggage and provisions: they have no hard labor, but have powerful enemies which keep them constantly on the watch and are never secure but in large camps. The manners and customs of all these tribes of the Plains, are much alike, and in giving those of the Peeagans, it may serve for all the others. Being the frontier tribe, they lead a more precarious and watchful life than other tribes, and from their boyhood are taught the use of arms, and to be good warriors, they became martial and more moral than the others, and many of them have a chivalrous bearing, ready for any enterprise. . . .

The Peeagans and their allies of the Plains, with us, would not be counted handsome. From infancy they are exposed to the weather and have not that softness of expression in their countenances which is so pleasing, but they are a fine race of men, tall and muscular, with manly features, and intelligent countenances, the eye large, black and piercing, the nose full and generally straight, the teeth regular and white, the hair long, straight and black; their beards, apparently would be equal to those of white men, did they not continually attempt to eradicate it; for when [they are] grown old and no longer pluck out the hairs they have more beard than could naturally be expected. Their color is something like that of a Spaniard from the south of Spain, and some like that of the French of the south of France, and this comparison is drawn from seeing them when bathing together. . . .

The Indians are noticed for their apathy, this is more assumed than real; in public he wishes it to appear that nothing can affect him, but in private he feels and expresses himself sensible to every thing that happens to him or to his family. After all his endeavours to attain some object in hunting, or other matters, and cannot do it, he says, the "Great Spirit will have it so," in the same manner as we say "It is the will of Providence." Civilized Men have many things to engage their attention and to take up their time, but the Indian is very different, hunting is his business, not his amusement, and even in this he is limited for want of ammunition hence his whole life is in the enjoyments of his passions, desires and affections contracted within a small circle, and in which it is often intense. . . .

The young men seldom marry before they are fully grown, about the age of 22 years or more, and the women about sixteen to eighteen. The older women who are related to them are generally the match makers, and the parties come together without any ceremony. On the marriage of the young men, two of them form a tent [household] until they have families, in which also reside the widowed

Mothers and Aunts. Polygamy is allowed and practised, and the Wife more frequently than her husband [is] the cause of it, for when a family comes a single wife can no longer do the duties and labor required unless she, or her husband, have two widowed relations in their tent, and which frequently is not the case; and a second wife is necessary, for they have to cook, take care of the meat, split and dry it; procure all the wood for fuel, dress the skins into soft leather for robes and clothing; which they have also to make and mend, and other duties which leaves scarce any part of the day to be idle, and in removing from place to place the taking down of the tents and putting them up are all performed by women. Some of the Chiefs have from three to six wives, for until a woman is near fifty years of age, she is sure to find a husband. A young Indian with whom I was acquainted and who was married often said, he would never have more than one wife, he had a small tent, and one of his aunts to help his wife; Nearly two years afterwards passing by where he was, I entered his tent, and [found] his first wife, as usual, sitting beside him, and on the other side three fine women in the prime of life, and as many elderly of the sex, in the back part. When I left the tent, he also came out, and telling me not to laugh at him for what he formerly said of having only one wife and he would explain to me how he had been obliged to take three more. "After I last saw you a friend of mine, whom I regarded and loved as a brother would go to war, he got wounded, returned, and shortly after died, relying on my friendship, when dying he requested his parents to send his two wives to me, where he was sure they would be kindly treated and become my wives. His parents brought them to me, with the dying request of my friend, what could I do but grant the claim of my friend, and make them my wives. Those are the two that sit next the door. The other one was the wife of a cousin who was also a friend of mine, he fell sick and died, and bequeathed his wife to my care. The old women at the back of the tent are their relations. I used to hunt the Antelopes, their skins make the finest leather for clothing, although the meat is not much, yet it is good and sufficient for us; but now I have given that over, and to maintain seven women and myself am obliged to confine myself to hunting the Red Deer and the Bison, which give us plenty of meat, tho' the leather is not so good. . . ."

The Indians of the Plains all punish adultery with death to both parties. This law does not appear to be founded on either religious, or moral, principles, but upon a high right of property as the best gift that Providence has given to them to be their wives and the mothers of their families; and without whom they cannot live. Every year there [are] some runaway matches between the young men and women; these are almost wholly from the hatred of the young women to polygamy. When a fine young woman, proud of herself, finds that instead of being given to her lover, she is to be the fourth, or fifth wife to some Man advanced in years, where she is to be the slave of the family, and bear all the bondage of a wife, without any of it's rights and priviledges, she readily consents to quit the camp with her lover, and go to some other camp at a distance where they have friends. In this case the affair is often made up, and the parents of the young woman are more pleased, than otherwise; yet it sometimes ends fatally. . . .

Poonokow (the Stag) was a son of the War Chief, Kootanae Appee. He was betrothed to a young woman, and only waited until the leather for a tent could be dressed to be a tent for them; during which, upon an insult from the Snake [Shoshoni] Indians, his father collected his Warriors to revenge it, and some of his sons accompanied him, among whom was Poonokow; the expedition was successful and he proudly returned with two fine horses one of which he intended for his father in law. During the expedition, by present and promises the father of another young man obtained her for his son. A friend went off [to] his fathers camp to inform him of the disposal of his intended bride, and [to tell him to] think no more of her, but his love for her was too strong to follow this advice. With his two horses he went near the camp, but did not enter it; here his friend parlied with him, whom he requested to send one of his aunts to him; she came, and he explained to her how he was dealt with and that he was determined to have his bride, tho' he should kill the man that had her. His aunt seeing his resolution, promised to speak to her and see what she would do, the young woman, as soon as she was informed of it, went to him, and they both set off for the Trading House on the Saskatchewan River, a journey of six days. When near the House, he saw a number of horses belonging to it, and not wishing to make his appearance on jaded horses, he unsaddled his own, and was putting the saddles on other two horses, when an Indian who was guarding them perceiving him and thinking he was stealing them shot him thro' the belly. He knew the wound was mortal, but had strength to reach the House, where he lay down and related what had passed; the next morning finding himself dying he took his sharp dagger in his hand, and held it ready to plunge into the heart of the young woman who had accompanied him and who was sitting beside him; he said to her, "Am I to go alone; do you really love me?" She burst into tears, held down her head, but said nothing. "I see you do not love me and I must go alone, tell my brother of what has happened and that I die by my own hand," then with his dagger [he] cut his belly from side to side, and with a hysteric laugh fell dead. The Traders buried him. The Peeagan young woman remained two days and as her fate appeared certain she was advised to go to some camp of the Blackfeet, but she refused, saying, he told me to go to his brothers, and to them I must go. And requesting a horse, which was given to her, with provisions, she went to the camp of the brothers of her deceased lover, and to them related the sad story; they pitied her, as they knew the Man to whom she was given would kill her, and told her so, and enquired what she intended to do. She said I know what I ought to have done, but my heart was weak, it is not so now; my life is gone, if I die by the hand of the man to whom I was given, I shall die a bad death, and in the other world wander friendless, and no one to take care of me; your brother loved me, he is in the other world, and will be kind to me and love me, have pity on me and send me to him; an arrow thro' her heart laid her dead, for her soul to rejoin her lover, and they buried her as the widow of their brother. Whatever may be the idea of some civilized atheists, the immortality of the soul is the high consolation of all the rude tribes of North America.

The character of all these people appear[s] to be brave, steady and deliberate, but on becoming acquainted with them there is no want of individual character, and almost every character in civilized society can be traced among them, from the gravity of a judge to a merry jester, and from open hearted generosity to the avaricious miser. This last character is more detested by them, than us, from their precarious manner of life, requiring assistance from each other, and their general character. Especially in provisions is great attention [paid] to those that are unfortunate in the chace, and the tent of a sick man is well supplied. . . .

The Natives of all these countries are fond of their children, they have faults like other children but are not corrected by being beat. Contempt and ridicule are the correctives employed, these shame them, without breaking their spirit. And as they are all brought up in the open camp, the other children help the punishment. . . .

The Peeagan in whose tent I passed the winter was an old man of at least 75 to 80 years of age; his height about six feet, two or three inches, broad shoulders, strong limbed, his hair gray and plentiful, forehead high and nose prominent, his face slightly marked with the small pox, and alltogether his countenance mild, and even, sometimes playfull; although his step was firm and he rode with ease, he no longer hunted, this he left to his sons; his name was Saukamappee (Young Man); his account of former times went back to about 1730 and was as follows.

The Peeagans were always the frontier Tribe, and upon whom the Snake [Shoshoni] Indians made their attacks, these latter were very numerous, even without their allies; and the Peeagans had to send messengers among us to procure help. Two of them came to the camp of my father, and I was then about his age (pointing to a Lad of about sixteen years) he promised to come and bring some of his people, the Nahathaways [Cree] with him, for I am myself of that people, and not of those with whom I am. My father brought about twenty warriors with him. There were a few guns amongst us, but very little ammunition, and they were left to hunt for the families; Our weapons was a Lance, mostly pointed with iron, some few of stone, A Bow and a quiver of Arrows; the Bows were of Larch, the length came to the chin; the quiver had about fifty arrows, of which ten had iron points, the others were headed with stone. He carried his knife on his breast and his axe in his belt. Such was my fathers weapons, and those with him had much of the same weapons. I had a Bow and Arrows and a knife, of which I was very proud. We came to the Peeagans and their allies. They were camped in the Plains on the left bank of the River (the north side) and were a great many. We were feasted, a great War Tent was made, and a few days passed in speeches, feasting and dances. A war chief was elected by the chiefs, and we got ready to march. Our spies had been out and had seen a large camp of the Snake Indians on the Plains of the Eagle Hill, and we had to cross the River in canoes, and on rafts, which we carefully secured for our retreat. When we had crossed and numbered our men, we were about 350 warriors (this he showed by counting every finger to be ten, and holding up both hands three times and then one hand) they had their scouts out, and came to meet us. Both parties made a great show of their numbers, and I thought that they were more numerous than ourselves.

After some singing and dancing, they sat down on the ground, and placed their large shields before them, which covered them: We did the same, but our shields were not so many, and some of our shields had to shelter two men. Theirs were all placed touching each other; their Bows were not so long as ours, but of better wood, and the back covered with the sinews of the Bisons which made them very elastic, and their arrows went a long way and whizzed about us as balls do from guns. They were all headed with a sharp smooth, black stone (flint) which broke when it struck anything. Our iron headed arrows did not go through their shields, but stuck in them; On both sides several were wounded, but none lay on the ground; and night put an end to the battle, without a scalp being taken on either side, and in those days such was the result, unless one party was more numerous than the other. The great mischief of war then, was as now, by attacking and destroying small camps of ten to thirty tents, which are obliged to separate for hunting: I grew to be a man, became a skilfull and fortunate hunter, and my relations procured me a Wife. She was young and handsome and we were fond of each other. We had passed a winter together, when Messengers came from our allies to claim assistance.

By this time the affairs of both parties had much changed; we had more guns and iron headed arrows than before; but our enemies the Snake Indians and their allies had Misstutim (Big Dogs, that is Horses) on which they rode, swift as the Deer, on which they dashed at the Peeagans, and with their stone [headed] Pukamoggan [club] knocked them on the head, and they had thus lost several of their best men. This news we did not well comprehend and it alarmed us, for we had no idea of Horses and could not make out what they were. Only three of us went and I should not have gone, had not my wife's relations frequently intimated, that her father's medicine bag would be honored by the scalp of a Snake Indian. When we came to our allies, the great War Tent [was made] with speeches, feasting and dances as before; and when the War Chief had viewed us all it was found between us and the Stone [Assiniboin] Indians we had ten guns and each of us about thirty balls, and powder for the war, and we were considered the strength of the battle. After a few days march our scouts brought us word that the enemy was near in a large war party, but had no Horses with them, for at that time they had very few of them. When we came to meet each other, as usual, each displayed their numbers, weapons and shiel[d]s, in all which they were superior to us, except our guns which were not shown, but kept in their leathern cases, and if we had shown [them], they would have taken them for long clubs. For a long time they held us in suspense; a tall Chief was forming a strong party to make an attack on our centre, and the others to enter into combat with those opposite to them; We prepared for the battle the best we could. Those of us who had guns stood in the front line, and each of us [had] two balls in his mouth, and a load of powder in his left hand to reload.

We noticed they had a great many short stone clubs for close combat, which is a dangerous weapon, and had they made a bold attack on us, we must have been defeated as they were more numerous and better armed than we were, for we could have fired our guns no more than twice; and were at a loss what to do on the wide plain, and each Chief encouraged his men to stand firm. Our eyes were all on the tall Chief and his motions, which appeared to be contrary to the advice of several old Chiefs, all this time we were about the strong flight of an arrow from each other. At length the tall chief retired and they formed their long usual line by placing their shields on the ground to touch each other, the shield having a breadth of full three feet or more. We sat down opposite to them and most of us waited for the night to make a hasty retreat. The War Chief was close to us, anxious to see the effect of our guns. The lines were too far asunder for us to make a sure shot, and we requested him to close the line to about sixty yards, which was gradually done, and lying flat on the ground behind the shields, we watched our opportunity when they drew their bows to shoot at us, their bodies were then exposed and each of us, as opportunity offered, fired with deadly aim, and either killed, or severely wounded, every one we aimed at.

The War Chief was highly pleased, and the Snake Indians finding so many killed and wounded kept themselves behind their shields; the War Chief then desired we would spread ourselves by two's throughout the line, which we did, and our shots caused consternation and dismay along their whole line. The battle had begun about Noon, and the Sun was not yet half down, when we perceived some of them had crawled away from their shields, and were taking to flight. The War Chief seeing this went along the line and spoke to every Chief to keep his Men ready for a charge of the whole line of the enemy, of which he would give the signal; this was done by himself stepping in front with his Spear, and calling on them to follow him as he rushed on their line, and in an instant the whole of us followed him, the greater part of the enemy took to flight, but some fought bravely and we lost more than ten killed and many wounded; Part of us pursued, and killed a few, but the chase had soon to be given over, for at the body of every Snake Indian killed, there were five or six of us trying to get his scalp, or part of his clothing, his weapons, or something as a trophy of the battle. As there were only three of us [Cree], and seven of our friends, the Stone Indians, we did not interfere, and got nothing.

The next morning the War Chief made a speech, praising their bravery, and telling them to make a large War Tent to commemorate their victory, to which they directly set to work and by noon it was finished.

The War Chief now called on all the other Chiefs to assemble their men and come to the Tent. In a short time they came, all those who had lost relations had their faces blackened; those who killed an enemy, or wished to be thought so, had their faces blackened with red streaks on the face, and those who had no pretensions to the one, or the other, had their faces red with ochre. We did not paint our faces until the War Chief told us to paint our foreheads and eyes black, and the rest of the face of dark red ochre, as having carried guns, and to distinguish us from all the rest. Those who had scalps now came forward with the scalps neatly stretched on a round willow with a handle to the frame; they appeared to be more than fifty, and excited loud shouts and the war whoop of victory. When this was over the War Chief told them that if any one had a right to the scalp of an enemy as a war trophy it ought to be us, who with our guns had gained the victory, when from the numbers of our enemies we were anxious to leave the field of battle; and that ten scalps must be given to us; this was soon collected, and he gave to each of us a Scalp. All those whose faces were blackened for the loss of relations, or friends, now came forward to claim the other scalps to be held in their hands for the benefit of their departed relations and friends; this occasioned a long conversation with those who had the scalps; at length they came forward to the War Chief, those who had taken the trophy from the head of the enemy they had killed, said the Souls of the enemy that each of us has slain, belong to us, and we have given them to our relations which are in the other world to be their slaves, and we are contented. Those who had scalps taken from the enemy that were found dead under the shields were at a loss what to say, as not one could declare he had actually slain the enemy whose scalp he held, and yet wanted to send their Souls to be the slaves of their departed relations. This caused much discussion; and the old Chiefs decided it could not be done, and that no one could send the soul of an enemy to be a slave in the other world, except the warriors who actually killed him; the scalps you hold are trophies of the Battle, but they give you no right to the soul of the enemy from whom it is taken, he alone who kills an enemy has a right to the soul, and to give it to be a slave to whom he pleases. This decision did not please them, but they were obliged to abide by it. The old Chiefs then turned to us, and praising our conduct in the battle said, each of you have slain two enemies in battle, if not more, you will return to your own people, and as you are young men, consult with the old men to whom you shall give the souls of those you have slain; until which let them wander about the other world. The Chiefs wished us to stay, and promised to each of us a handsome young wife, and [to] adopt us as their sons, but we told them we were anxious to see our relations and people, after which, perhaps we might come back. After all the war ceremonies were over, we pitched away in large camps with the women and children on the frontier of the Snake Indian country, hunting the Bison and Red Deer which were numerous, and we were anxious to see a horse of which we had heard so much. At last, as the leaves were falling we heard that one was killed by an arrow shot into his belly, but the Snake Indian that rode him, got away; numbers of us went to see him, and we all admired him, he put us in mind of a Stag that had lost his horns; and we did not know what name to give him. But as he was a slave to Man, like the dog, which carried our things; he was named the Big Dog.

We set off for our people [the Cree], . . . My mind was wholly bent on making a grand appearance before my Wife and her Parents, and presenting to her father the scalp I had to ornament his Medicine Bag: and before we came to the camp we had dressed ourselves, and painted each other's faces to appear to the best advantage, and were proud of ourselves. On seeing some of my friends I got away and went to them, and by enquiries learned that my parents had gone to the low countries of the Lakes, and that before I was three Moons away my wife had given herself to another man, and that her father could not prevent her, and they were all to the northward there to pass the winter.

At this unlooked for news I was quite disheartened; I said nothing, but my heart was swollen with anger and revenge, and I passed the night scheming mischief. In the morning my friends reasoned with me upon my vexation about a worthless woman, and that it was beneath a warrior anger, there were no want of women to replace her, and a better wife could be got. Others said, that if I had staid with my wife instead of running away to kill Snake Indians, nothing of this would have happened. My anger moderated, I gave my Scalp to one of my friends to give to my father, and renouncing my people, I left them, and came to the Peeagans who gave me a hearty welcome; and upon my informing them of my intention to remain with them the great Chief gave me his eldest daughter to be my wife, she is the sister of the present Chief, and as you see, now an old woman.

The terror of that battle and of our guns has prevented any more general battles, and our wars have since been carried by ambuscade and surprise, of small camps, in which we have greatly the advantage, from the Guns, arrow shods of iron, long knives, flat bayonets and axes from the Traders. While we have these weapons, the Snake

Indians have none, but what few they sometimes take from one of our small camps which they have destroyed, and they have no Traders among them. We thus continued to advance through the fine plains to the Stag River when death came over us all, and swept away more than half of us by the Small pox, of which we knew nothing until it brought death among us. We caught it from the Snake Indians. Our Scouts were out for our security, when some returned and informed us of a considerable camp which was too large to attack and something very suspicious about it; from a high knowl [sic] they had a good view of the camp, but saw none of the men hunting, or going about; there were a few Horses, but no one came to them, and a herd of Bisons [were] feeding close to the camp with other herds near. This somewhat alarmed us as a stratagem of War; and our Warriors thought this camp had a larger not far off; so that if this camp was attacked which was strong enough to offer a desperate resistance, the other would come to their assistance and overpower us as had been once done by them, and in which we lost many of our men.

The council ordered the Scouts to return and go beyond this camp, and be sure there was no other. In the mean time we advanced our camp; The scouts returned and said no other tents were near, and the camp appeared in the same state as before. Our Scouts had been going too much about their camp and were seen; they expected what would follow, and all those that could walk, as soon as night came on, went away. Next morning at the dawn of day, we attacked the Tents, and with our sharp flat daggers and knives, cut through the tents and entered for the fight; but our war whoop instantly stopt, our eyes were appalled with terror; there was no one to fight with but the dead and the dying, each a mass of corruption. We did not touch them, but left the tents, and held a council on what was to be done. We all thought the Bad Spirit had made himself master of the camp and destroyed them. It was agreed to take some of the best of the tents, and any other plunder that was clean and good, which we did, and also took away the few Horses they had, and returned to our camp.

The second day after this dreadful disease broke out in our camp, and spread from one tent to another as if the Bad Spirit carried it. We had no belief that one Man could give it to another, any more than a wounded Man could give his wound to another. We did not suffer so much as those that were near the river, into which they rushed and died. We had only a little brook, and about one third of us died, but in some of the other camps there were tents in which every one died. When at length it left us, and we moved about to find our people, it was no longer with the song and the dance; but with tears, shrieks, and howlings of despair for those who would never return to us. War was no longer thought of, and we had enough to do to hunt and make provision for our families, for in our sickness we had consumed all our dried provisions; but the Bisons and Red Deer were also gone, we did not see one half of what was before, whither they had gone we could not tell, we believed the Good Spirit had forsaken us, and allowed the Bad Spirit to become our Master. What little we could spare we offered to the Bad Spirit to let us alone and go to our enemies. To the Good Spirit we offered feathers, branches of trees, and sweet smelling grass. Our hearts were low and dejected, and we shall never be again the same people. To hunt for our families was our sole occupation and kill Beavers, Wolves and Foxes to trade our necessaries; and we thought of War no more, and perhaps would have made peace with them for they had suffered dreadfully as well as us and had left all this fine country of the Bow River to us.

# 5 / THE SELF-ASSERTIVE NOOTKA OF BRITISH COLUMBIA

*The Nootka belonged to the Northwest Coast culture area. Although none of the peoples in this area farmed, nature produced a supply of fish and sea mammals which was inexhaustible by the techniques the Indians employed in taking them. The actual surplus of food in this area made it possible for these Indians to develop a number of things generally associated with farming societies. For instance, they lived in large plank houses in permanent villages with relatively heavy concentration of population in small areas, had slaves, made careful distinctions in the rank of freemen, possessed secret societies, and had a well-developed pattern of war raids aimed at capturing anything of value, including people to be converted into slaves.*

*It was by such people that John R. Jewitt was taken prisoner at age nineteen in the year 1802. Jewitt's life was spared because he was the ship's armourer and had luckily repaired the chief's gun on the day before the massacre of the ship's crew. Jewitt also saved the life of a man named Thompson by insisting that Thompson was his father. The massacre was not unprovoked, as the Nootka Indians had suffered loss of life at the hands of the crews of previous European ships. Jewitt and Thompson became slaves of the chief in the beginning but, after both distinguished themselves in a war raid and Jewitt married an Indian wife, they gained the status of*

John R. Jewitt, *A Narrative of the Adventures and Sufferings of John R. Jewitt* (Middletown, Conn.: Printed by Loomis and Richards, 1815), pp. 61-64, 68-72, 87-89, 135-37, 147-50, 153-59, 170-72, 176-78, 189-90, 197.

*freemen and even owned a few slaves themselves. This freedom, however, did not include the freedom to contact the next ship that came along and return to England.*

*However, they maneuvered themselves into a position that made rescue possible in 1805 without any loss of life on either side.*

*Although Juan Perez anchored in Nootka Sound in 1774 and allowed a few Indians to board his ship, he sailed away without any of his crew's touching foot on shore. Captain James Cook wintered in the same sound in 1778 and made a few observations on the natives on shore. Other ships stopped to trade for furs at later dates in the same century, but Jewitt was the first White man actually to live with these Indians, and his observations are fuller than those of any of his predecessors.*

The houses as I have observed are above twenty in number, built nearly in a line. These are of different sizes according to the rank or quality of the *Tyee*, or chief, who lives in them, each having one, of which he is considered as the lord. They vary not much in width being usually from thirty-six to forty feet wide but are of very different lengths, that of the king which is much the longest being about one hundred and fifty feet, while the smallest which contain only two families do not exceed forty feet in length, the house of the king is also distinguished from the others by being higher.

Their method of building, is as follows, they erect in the ground two very large posts at such a distance apart as is intended for the length of the house. On these, which are of equal height, and hollowed out at the upper end, they lay a large spar for the ridgepole of the building, or if the length of the house requires it, two or more, supporting their ends by similar upright posts; these spars are sometimes of an almost incredible size, having myself measured one in Maquina's [the chief's] house which I found to be one hundred feet long and eight feet four inches in circumference. . . . The roof is formed of pine planks. . . . On these they lay large stones to prevent their being displaced by the wind. . . . The sides of their houses are much more open and exposed to the weather, . . . being built with planks of about ten feet long and four or five wide, which they place between stancheons or small posts of the height of the roof. . . . The planks or boards which they make use of for building their houses, and for other uses, they procure of different lengths as occasion requires, by splitting them out, with hard wooden wedges from pine logs, and afterwards dubbing them down with their chizzels, with much patience, to the thickness wanted, rendering them quite smooth.

There is but one entrance; this is placed usually at the end, though sometimes in the middle as was that of Maquina's. Through the middle of the building from one end to the other, runs a passage of about eight or nine feet broad, on each side of which, the several families that occupy it, live, each having its particular fire place, but without any kind of wall or separation to mark their respective limits; the chief having his apartment at the upper end, and the next in rank opposite on the other side. They have no other floor than the ground; the fire place or hearth consists of a number of stones loosely put together, but they are wholly without a chimney, nor is there any opening left in the roof, but whenever a fire is made, the plank immediately over it is thrust aside, by means of a pole, to give vent to the smoke. The height of the houses in general, from the ground to the center of the roof does not exceed ten feet, that of Maquina's was not far from fourteen; the spar forming the ridgepole of the latter was painted in red and black circles alternately by way of ornament, and the large posts that supported it had their tops curiously wrought or carved, so as to represent human heads of a monstrous size, which were painted in their manner. These were not, however, considered as objects of adoration, but merely as ornaments. . . .

Their mode of living is very simple—their food consisting almost wholly of fish, or fish spawn fresh or dried, the blubber of the whale, seal, or sea-cow, muscles, clams, and berries of various kinds; all of which are eaten with a profusion of train oil for sauce, not excepting even the most delicate fruit, as strawberries and raspberries. With so little variety in their food, no great can be expected, in their cookery. Of this, indeed, they may be said to know but two methods, viz. by boiling and steaming, and even the latter is not very frequently practised by them. Their mode of boiling is as follows: into one of their tubs, they pour water sufficient to cook the quantity of provision wanted. A number of heated stones are then put in to make it boil. . . .

When they cook their fish by steam, which are usually the heads, tails, and fins of the salmon, cod and halibut, a large fire is kindled, upon which they place a bed of stones, which, when the wood is burnt down, becomes perfectly heated. Layers of green leaves or pine boughs, are then placed upon the stones, and the fish, clams, &c. being laid upon them, water is poured over them, and the whole closely covered with mats to keep in the steam. This is much the best mode of cooking, and clams and muscles done in this manner, are really excellent. . . .

Whenever a feast is given by the king or any of the chiefs, there is a person who acts as a master of ceremonies, and whose business it is to receive the guests as they enter the house and point out to them their respective seats which is regulated with great punctiliousness as regards rank; the king occupying the highest or the seat of honour, his son or brother sitting next him, and so on with the chiefs according to their quality; the private persons belonging to the same family being always placed together to prevent any confusion. The women are seldom invited to their feasts, and only at those times when a general invitation is given to the village.

As whenever they cook, they always calculate to have an abundance for all the guests, a profusion in this respect being considered as the highest luxury, much more is usually set before them than they can eat. That which is left in the king's tray he sends to his house for his family, by one of his slaves, as do the chiefs theirs, while those who eat from the same tray and who generally belong to the same family, take it home as common stock, or each one receives his portion, which is distributed on the spot. This custom appeared very singular to my companion and myself, and it was a most awkward thing for us at first, to have to lug home with us, in our hands or arms, the blubber or fish that we received at these times, but we soon became reconciled to it, and were very glad of an opportunity to do it. . . .

Their slaves, as I have observed, form their most valuable species of property. These are of both sexes, being either captives taken by themselves in war, or purchased from the neighboring tribes, and who reside in the same house, forming as it were a part of the family, are usually kindly treated, eat of the same food, and live as well as their masters. They are compelled however at times to labour severely, as not only all the menial offices are performed by them, such as bringing water, cutting wood and a variety of others, but they are obliged to make the canoes, to assist in building and repairing the houses, to supply their masters with fish, and to attend them to war and to fight for them. None but the king and chiefs have slaves, the common people being prevented from holding them either from their inability to purchase them, or as I am the rather inclined to think from its being considered as the privilege of the former alone to have them, especially as all those made prisoners in war belong either to the king or the chiefs, who have captured them, each one holding such as have been taken by himself or his slaves. There is probably however some little distinction in favor of the king, who is always the commander of the expedition, as Maquina had nearly fifty, male and female, in his house, a number constituting about one half of its inhabitants, comprehending those obtained by war and purchase, whereas none of the other chiefs had more than twelve. The females are employed principally in manufacturing cloth, in cooking, collecting berries, &c. and with regard to food and living in general have not a much harder lot than their mistresses, the principal difference consisting, in these poor unfortunate creatures being considered as free to any one, their masters prostituting them whenever they think proper for the purpose of gain. In this way many of them are brought on board the ships and offered to the crews, from whence an opinion appears to have been formed by some of our navigators, injurious to the chastity of their females, than which nothing can be more generally untrue, as perhaps in no part of the world is that virtue more prized. . . .

As these people have some very singular observances preparatory to whaling, an account of them will, I presume, not prove uninteresting, especially as it may serve to give a better idea of their manners. A short time before leaving Tashees, the king makes a point of passing a day alone on the mountain, whither he goes very privately early in the morning, and does not return till late in the evening. This is done, as I afterwards learned, for the purpose of singing and praying to his God for success in whaling the ensuing season. At Cooptee the same ceremony is performed, and at Nootka after the return thither, with still greater solemnity, as for the next two days he appears very thoughtful and gloomy, scarcely speaking to any one, and observes a most rigid fast. On these occasions, he has always a broad red fillet made of bark, bound around his head, in token of humiliation, with a large branch of green spruce on the top, and his great rattle in his hand. In addition to this, for a week before commencing their whaling, both himself and the crew of his canoe observe a fast, eating but very little, and going into the water several times in the course of each day to bathe, singing and rubbing their bodies, limbs and faces with shells and bushes, so that on their return I have seen them look as though they had been severely torn with briers. They are likewise obliged to abstain from any commerce with their women for the like period, the latter restriction being considered as indispensible to their success.

Early in June Tootoosch, the crazy chief, died. On being acquainted with his death the whole village, men, women, and children set up a loud cry, with every testimony of the greatest grief, which they continued for more than three hours. As soon as he was dead, the body, according to their custom, was laid out on a plank, having the head bound round with a red bark fillet, which is with them an emblem of mourning and sorrow. After laying some time in this manner, he was wrapped in an otter skin robe, and three fathoms of I-whaw being put about his neck, he was placed in a large coffin or box of about three feet deep, which was ornamented on the outside with two rows of the small white shells. In this, the most valuable articles of his property were placed with him, among which were no less than twenty four prime sea-otter skins. At night, which is their time for interring the dead, the coffin was borne by eight men with two poles, thrust through ropes passed around it, to the place of burial, accompanied by his wife and family, with their hair cut short, in token of grief, all the inhabitants joining the procession. The place of burial was a large cavern on the side of a hill at a little distance from the village, in which, after depositing the coffin carefully, all the attendants repaired to Maquina's house, where a number of articles belonging to the deceased, consisting of blankets, pieces of cloth, &c. were burned by a person appointed by Maquina for that purpose, dressed and painted in the highest style, with his head covered with white down, who, as he put in the several pieces, one by one, poured upon them a quantity of oil to increase the flame, in the intervals between, making a speech and playing off a variety of buffoon tricks, and the whole closed with a feast, and a dance from Sat-sat-sak-sis, the king's son. . . .

When these people, have finally determined on war, they make it an invariable practise for three or four weeks prior to the expedition, to go into the water five or six times a day, when they wash and scrub themselves from head to foot with bushes intermixed with briars, so that their bodies and faces will often be entirely covered with blood. During this severe exercise, they are continually exclaiming, *"Wocash Qauhootze, Teechamme ah welth, wik-etish tauilth—Kar-sab-matemas—Wik-sish to hauk matemas—I ya-ish kah-shittle—As-smootish warich matemas*—Which signifies, Good, or great God, let me live—Not be sick—Find the enemy—Not fear him—Find him asleep, and kill a great many of him.

During the whole of this period, they have no intercourse with their women, and for a week, at least, before setting out abstain from feasting or any kind of merriment, appearing thoughtful, gloomy, and morose, and for the three last days, are almost constantly in the water, both by day and night, scrubbing and lacerating themselves in a terrible manner. Maquina having informed Thompson [the other captive Englishman] and myself that he should take us with him, was very solicitous that we should bathe and scrub ourselves in the same way with them, telling me that it would harden our skins so that the weapons of the enemy would not pierce them, but as we felt no great inclination to amuse ourselves in this manner, we declined it.

The expedition consisted of forty canoes, carrying from ten to twenty men each. Thompson and myself armed ourselves with cutlasses and pistols, but the natives, although they had a plenty of European arms, took with them only their daggers and cheetoolths, with a few bows and arrows, the latter being about a yard in length, and pointed with copper, muscle shell or bone: the bows are four feet and a half long, with strings made of whale sinew.

To go to A-y-chart [the enemy village], we ascended from twenty to thirty miles, a river about the size of that of Tashees, the banks of which are high and covered with wood. At midnight, we came in sight of the village, which was situated on the west bank near the shore, on a steep hill difficult of access, and well calculated for defence. It consisted of fifteen or sixteen houses, smaller than those at Nootka, and built in the same style, but compactly placed. By Maquina's directions, the attack was deferred until the first appearance of dawn, as he said that was the time when men slept the soundest.

At length all being ready for the attack, we landed with the greatest silence, and going around so as to come upon the foe in the rear, clambered up the hill, and while the natives, as is their custom, entered the several huts, creeping on all fours, my comrade and myself stationed ourselves without, to intercept those who should attempt to escape, or come to the aid of their friends. I wished if possible, not to stain my hands in the blood of any fellow creature, and though Thompson would gladly have put to death all the savages in the country, he was too brave to think of attacking a sleeping enemy. Having entered the houses, on the war-whoop being given by Maquina, as he seized the head of the chief, and gave him a fatal blow, all proceeded to the work of death. The A-y-charts being thus surprised, were unable to make resistance, and with the exception of a very few, who were so fortunate as to make their escape, were all killed or taken prisoners on condition of becoming slaves to their captors. I had the good fortune to take four captives, whom Maquina, as a favor, permitted me to consider as mine, and occasionally employ them in fishing for me; as for Thompson, who thirsted for revenge, he had no wish to take any prisoners, but with his cutlass, the only weapon he would employ against them, succeeded in killing seven stout fellows, who came to attack him, an act which obtained him great credit with Maquina and the chiefs, who after this, held him in much higher estimation, and gave him the appellation of *Chehiel-suma-har,* it being the name of a very celebrated warrior of their nation in ancient times, whose exploits were the constant theme of their praise. . . .

Soon after our establishment there, Maquina informed me, that he and his chiefs had held council both before and after quitting Nootka, in which they had determined that I must marry one of their women. . . . Reduced to this sad extremity, with death on the one side, and matrimony on the other, I thought proper to choose what appeared to me the least of the two evils, and consent to be married, on condition, that as I did not fancy any of the

Nootka women, I should be permitted to make choice of one from some other tribe.

This being settled, the next morning by day light Maquina with about fifty men in two canoes, set out with me for A-i-tiz-zart, taking with him a quantity of cloth, a number of muskets, sea otter skins, &c. for the purchase of my bride. With the aid of our paddles and sails, being favoured with a fair breeze, we arrived some time before sun set at the village. Our arrival excited a general alarm, and the men hastened to the shore, armed with the weapons of their country, making many warlike demonstrations, and displaying much zeal and activity. We in the mean time remained quietly seated in our canoes, where we remained for about half an hour, when the messenger of the chief, dressed in their best manner, came to welcome us and invite us on shore to eat. We followed him in procession to the chief's house, Maquina at our head, taking care to leave a sufficient number in the boats to protect the property. When we came to the house, we were ushered in with much ceremony, and our respective seats pointed out to us, mine being next to Maquina by his request.

After having been regaled with a feast of herring spawn and oil, Maquina asked me if I saw any among the women who were present that I liked, I immediately pointed out to him a young girl of about seventeen, the daughter of *Upquesta,* the chief, who was sitting near him by her mother. On this Maquina making a sign to his men, arose and taking me by the hand, walked into the middle of the room, and sent off two of his men to bring the boxes containing the presents from the canoes. . . . When the chests were brought in, specimens of the several articles were taken out, and shewed by our men, one of whom held up a musket, another a skin, a third a piece of cloth, &c. On this, Kinneclimmets stepped forward, and addressing the chief, informed him that all these belonged to me, mentioning the number of each kind, and that they were offered him for the purchase of his daughter *Eu-stoch-ee-exqua,* as a wife for me. . . . Maquina [then] rose, and in a speech of more than half an hour, said much in my praise to the A-i-tiz-zart chief. . . .

When he had ceased, the A-i-tiz-zart chief arose amidst the acclamations of his people, and began with setting forth the many good qualities and accomplishments of his daughter; that he loved

her greatly, and as she was his only one, he could not think of parting with her. He spoke in this manner for some time, but finally
concluded by consenting to the proposed union, requesting that she
might be well used and kindly treated by her husband. . . .

When Upquesta had finished his speech, he directed his people to
carry back the presents which Maquina had given him, to me, together with two young male slaves to assist me in fishing. . . .

In the morning I received from the chief his daughter, with an
earnest request that I would use her well, which I promised him,
when taking leave of her parents, she accompanied me with apparent satisfaction on board of the canoe. . . .

At about five in the morning, we reached Tashees, where we
found all the inhabitants collected on the shore to receive us. We
were welcomed with loud shouts of joy, and exclamations of Wocash, and the women taking my bride under their charge, conducted her to Maquina's house, to be kept with them for ten days;
it being an universal custom, as Maquina informed me, that no
intercourse should take place between the new married pair during
that period. At night Maquina gave a great feast, which was succeeded by a dance, in which all the women joined, and thus ended
the festivities of my marriage. . . .

The office of king or chief, is, with those people, hereditary, and
descends to the eldest son, or in failure of male issue, to the elder
brother, who in the regal line, is considered as the second person
in the kingdom. At feasts, as I have observed, the king is always
placed in the highest, or seat of honour, and the chiefs according
to their respective ranks, which appear, in general, to be determined
by their affinity to the royal family, they are also designated by the
embellishments of their mantles, or Kutsaks. The king, or head
Tyee, is their leader in war, in the management of which he is perfectly absolute. He is also president of their councils, which are
almost always regulated by his opinion. But he has no kind of power
over the property of his subjects, nor can he require them to contribute to his wants, being in this respect, no more privileged than
any other person. He has in common with his chiefs, the right of
holding slaves, which is not enjoyed by private individuals, a regu-
lation probably arising from their having been originally captives
taken in battle, the spoils of war being understood as appertaining

to the king, who receives and apportions them among his several chiefs and warriors, according to their rank and desert. In conformity with this idea, the plunder of the [ship] Boston, was all deposited in Maquina's house, who distributed part of it among his chiefs, according to their respective ranks or degree of favour with him, giving to one, three hundred muskets, to another, one hundred and fifty, with other things in like proportion. The king is, however, obliged to support his dignity by making frequent entertainments, and whenever he receives a large supply of provision, he must invite all the men of his tribe to his house, to eat it up, otherwise, as Maquina told me, he would not be considered as conducting like a Tyee, and would be no more thought of than a common man.

With regard to their religion——They believe in the existence of a Supreme Being, whom they call *Quahootze,* and who, to use Maquina's expression, was one great Tyee in the sky, who gave them their fish, and could take them from them, and was the greatest of all kings. Their usual place of worship, appeared to be the water, for whenever they bathed, they addressed some words in form of prayer to the God above, intreating that he would preserve them in health, give them good success in fishing, &c. These prayers were repeated with much more energy, on preparing for whaling or for war, as I have already mentioned. Some of them would sometimes go several miles to bathe, in order to do it in secret, the reason for this I could never learn, though I am induced to think it was in consequence of some family or private quarrel, and that they did not wish what they said to be heard; while at other times, they would repair in the same secret manner to the woods, to pray. This was more particularly the case with the women, who might also, have been prompted by a sentiment of decency, to retire for the purpose of bathing, as they are remarkably modest. I once found one of our women more than two miles from the village, on her knees in the woods, with her eyes shut, and her face turned towards heaven, uttering words in a lamentable tone, among which I distinctly heard, *Wocash Ah-welth,* meaning good Lord, and which has nearly the same signification with Quahootze. Though I came very near her, she appeared not to notice me, but continued her devotions, and I have frequently seen the women go alone into the woods, evidently for the purpose of addressing themselves to a superior being, and it was always very perceptible on their return, when they had been thus employed, from their silence and melancholy looks. . . .

The Nootkians in their conduct towards each other, are in general pacific and inoffensive, and appear by no means an illtempered race, for I do not recollect any instance of a violent quarrel between any of the men, or the men and their wives, while I was with them, that of Yaelthlower excepted. But when they are in the least offended, they appear to be in the most violent rage, acting like so many maniacs, foaming at the mouth, kicking and spitting most furiously; but this is rather a fashion with them, than a demonstration of malignity, as in their public speeches, they use the same violence, and he is esteemed the greatest orator, who bawls the loudest, stamps, tosses himself about, foams and spits the most. . . .

It was now past mid-summer, and the hopes we had indulged of our release, became daily more faint, for though we had heard of no less than seven vessels on the coast, yet none appeared inclined to venture to Nootka. The destruction of the Boston, the largest, strongest, and best equipped ship, with much the most valuable cargo of any that had ever been fitted out for the North West trade, had inspired the commanders of others with a general dread of coming thither, lest they share the same fate; . . . on the morning of the nineteenth of July . . . my ears were saluted with the joyful sound of three cannon, and the cries of the inhabitants, exclaiming, Weena, weena—Mamethlee—that is, strangers—white men.

Soon after several of our people, came running into the house, to inform me that a vessel under full sail was coming into the harbour. Though my heart bounded with joy, I repressed my feelings, and affecting to pay no attention to what was said, told Thompson to be on his guard, and not betray any joy, as our release, and perhaps our lives, depended on our conducting ourselves so as to induce the natives to suppose we were not very anxious to leave them. . . .

With feelings of joy impossible to be described, did I quit this savage shore, confident now that nothing could thwart my escape, or prevent the execution of the plan I had formed. . . .

Notwithstanding my joy at my deliverance, and the pleasing anticipation I felt of once more beholding a civilized country, and again being permitted to offer up my devotions in a Christian church, I could not avoid experiencing a painful sensation on parting with this savage chief, who had preserved my life, and in general treated me with kindness, and considering their ideas and manners, much better than could have been expected.

# II / INTERMEDIATE FARMING CULTURES

## 6 / THE CANNIBALISTIC TUPINAMBA OF BRAZIL

*The Tupinamba lived in several localities on the east coast of Brazil between the mouth of the Amazon River and Rio de Janeiro. Among them were found warfare and cannibalism with all the trimmings. This bloodthirsty pattern was most strongly developed around the Caribbean Sea, but also occurred in parts of Brazil, in Mexico, and in the eastern United States. The term savage, no longer used by anthropologists, is, nevertheless, not inappropriate for these peoples, who fortunately formed a minority in the New World as a whole. The Tupinamba derived the principal part of their subsistence from farming, and the women did both the planting and harvesting. The men spent most of their time and energy hunting and fighting. The popular notion that the most bloodthirsty peoples should be found among the hunters, gatherers, and fishers, rather than among those in higher economic levels, is not only contradicted by the Tupinamba but is generally false for the Americas. All the peoples in the areas where this pattern prevailed, cited above, were farmers, and the Aztecs fall in the group of advanced farming cultures. Most Indians were more humane and peaceful, one of the most peaceful in this volume being the Zuñi. The author of this selection on the Tupinamba, Alfred Métraux, has read all the original sixteenth-century Portuguese sources and has carefully combined them in this succinct sketch of their social, political, and religious life.*

Alfred Métraux, "The Tupinamba," *Handbook of South American Indians,* Julian H. Steward, ed., Bureau of American Ethnology, Bulletin 143, III (1948), 111-26.

Like many Guiana Indians, they lived in large communal houses, whose occupants were related either by blood or by marriage and were probably the members of a patrilineal extended family. A man's brother's daughter was regarded as his daughter, but his sister's daughter was his potential wife. The children of a woman of the tribe by a captive father were regarded as members of the enemy group and were consequently eaten by their mother's relatives. The children of a tribesman were always full-fledged members of the community irrespective of the mother's status. . . .

A man with several daughters attained considerable authority and prestige because he had under him both his sons-in-law and his daughters' suitors. Men who had changed names often, having killed several enemies in battle or sacrificed captives on the village plaza, acquired great prestige and influence in the community.

Though, with few exceptions, all prisoners, male or female, were eventually eaten, they were kept long enough in the community to be considered a special class within *Tupinamba* society. Possession of a prisoner was an envied privilege. One who enjoyed it did not hesitate to make the greatest sacrifices to keep his charge happy and in good health. A man would starve rather than deprive his captive of food, and usually gave him a daughter or sister as a wife. Lacking a close female relative, the captor would ask a friend to give him a woman for the purpose, a request sure to be granted, for conjugal ties with a prisoner were regarded as honorable. In certain cases the prisoner was married to the widow of a warrior killed before his capture and was allotted the deceased's hammock and ornaments. The relations between a prisoner and his new wife were identical with those of any other married couple and were supposed to last forever, the woman being just as attached to her temporary husband as in normal wedlock. These prisoners' wives, it is said, had the responsibility of preventing their husbands from running away, but the statement is to be accepted with reserve. Some authors report cases of women who grew so fond of their husbands that they escaped with them.

Female captives were often taken as secondary wives or concubines by their masters, but sooner or later they were ritually sacrificed unless they belonged to an influential man who had become fond of them. If their masters did not care for them, they were allowed to have sexual relations with whomever they wished. The skulls of female captives who died a natural death were crushed. Prisoners were kindly treated and regarded their masters, whose quarters they shared, as relatives. The *Tupinamba* were heartbroken to see Europeans mistreat the prisoners they had sold to them. They would come from far away to visit them, and would hide and protect any of their former slaves who escaped. . . .

Each long house had a headman who was under the village chief. Some villages had two or even three or four chiefs, if we may rely on Claude d'Abbeville's census of the Maranhao region. Some chiefs extended their power over a whole district and commanded a great many villages. Rank was determined by war prowess (capture and ceremonial execution of prisoners), magic power, oratorical gifts, and wealth.

Soares de Souza writes:

> The chief must be a man of courage. He has to belong to a large family and to be well liked by its members so that they are willing to help cultivate his plantations, but even when he opens a clearing with the assistance of relatives, he is the first to put his hand to the task. (Soares de Souza, 1851, p. 325.)

The authority of chiefs, undisputed in war time, was subordinated to the sanction of a council in peace.

This council was composed of the elder men and famous warriors, who met on the village plaza for any important decision. The chief spoke first, and then each councilor in turn gave his opinion, while the others, according to their rank, sat in their hammocks or squatted on the ground smoking huge cigarettes.

Each morning the headman of a hut assigned everybody a task and delivered a speech encouraging the people to go to work and follow the good example of their ancestors.

Chieftainship was inherited by the son or the brother of the deceased chief, if he had the required qualifications.

Social control over the individual's behavior was very strong. Great stress was put on the smoothness of manners and gentleness, any outburst of anger being looked on with abhorrence. People shunned the company of temperamental persons. If an Indian felt incapable of controlling his feelings, he warned those present, who immediately tried to calm him down. When a serious quarrel broke out in a village, the individuals involved went to the extreme of burning their own houses, challenging their adversaries to do likewise. Under the influence of anger, these Indians were prone to commit suicide by eating soil.

Blood revenge was a sacred duty. When a homicide might involve two allied groups in a feud, the relatives of the murderer often did not hesitate to kill him, lest the peace be disturbed. . . .

After death the souls of gallant warriors killed in battle or eaten by their enemies went to a beautiful land in the west where they enjoyed the company of the mythical "grandfather" and of their dead ancestors. They lived there happily and made merry forever. Access to this paradise was forbidden to cowards and to women, except the wives of renowned warriors.

Religious and social values of high importance clustered around war and the closely connected practice of cannibalism. Prestige and political power were derived mainly from the ritual slaughtering of prisoners, which was so far reaching in its influence that it even affected sexual life. The *Tupinamba's* excessive interest in ritual cannibalism contributed toward keeping the different tribes and even local communities in a constant state of warfare and was one of the chief causes of their ready subjection by Europeans. Their mutual hatred of one another, born of a desire to avenge the insult of cannibalism, was so great that the *Tupinamba* groups always willingly marched with the White invaders against their local rivals. Their bellicose disposition and craving for human flesh loom large in many aspects of their culture, such as education, oratory, poetry, and religion. The rites and festivities that marked the execution of a prisoner and the consumption of his body were joyful events which provided these Indians with the opportunity for merrymaking, esthetic displays, and other emotional outlets.

The *Tupinamba* went to war only with the certainty of victory, which they derived from the interpretation of dreams and from ritualistic performances such as dancing and reciting charms. When marching toward the enemy, they paid special attention to any omen and to dreams. The slightest bad omen was sufficient to stop the expedition: once a party of warriors that had almost taken a village retreated because of a few words uttered by a parrot.

Besides arrows and bows, *Tupinamba* weapons included a hardwood club with a shape unique in South America. It consisted of two parts: a long, rounded handle and a flattened, round, or oval blade with sharp edges. The only defensive weapon was a shield of tapir hide. Warriors donned their best feather ornaments and painted their bodies. Men of importance were followed by their wives, who carried hammocks and food for them. The advancing army was accompanied by musical instruments. Whenever possible, they used canoes to avoid long marches. The chief always headed the column, which was disposed in one line. Scouts reconnoitered the country. At night the warriors camped near a river and built small huts in a row along a path.

The proper time to assault the enemy village was chosen cautiously. As a rule, they stormed it at night or at dawn, when least expected. When prevented by a stockade from entering a village immediately, they built another palisade of thorny bushes around the village and started a siege. One tactic was to set fire to the enemy houses with incendiary arrows. Sometimes they slowly moved their fence close to the opposite wall so that they could fight at close range.

The *Tupinamba* fought with courage and determination but without much order as they did not obey any command during the battle. They opened the attack by shooting arrows, hopping about with great agility from one spot to another to prevent the enemy from aiming or shooting at any definite individual. Amid ferocious howls, they rushed against their opponents to strike them with their clubs, trying to take prisoners, one of the main purposes of the war. Because it was difficult to seize an enemy without the assistance of several persons, it was an established rule that the prisoner belonged to the first man to touch him. When a man was disarmed, the victor touched him on the shoulder and said, "You are my prisoner." Thereafter, the man was his slave. Those who remained in possession of the battlefield would roast the corpses and bring back the heads and the sexual organs of the dead.

The long set of cannibalistic rites and practices began immediately after the capture of a prisoner. On the way home, the victorious party exhibited their captives in friendly villages, where they were subjected to "gross insults and vituperation." The latter retaliated by expressing their contempt for their victors and their pride at being eaten as befitted the brave.

Before entering their masters' village, the prisoners were dressed as *Tupinamba,* with foreheads shaven, feathers glued to their bodies, and a decoration of feather ornaments. They were taken to the graves of the recently deceased of the community and compelled to "renew," that is, clean them. Later they received the hammocks, ornaments, and weapons of the dead, which had to be used before they could be reappropriated by the heirs. The reason for this custom was that touching the belongings of a dead relative was fraught with danger, unless they were first defiled by a captive.

When the prisoners were taken into the village, women flocked around them, snatched them from the hands of the men, and accompanied them, celebrating their capture with songs, dances, and references to the day of their execution. They forced the prisoners to dance in front of the hut where the sacred rattles were kept.

After this hostile reception, the prisoners' condition changed for the better. Their victors often gave them to a son or some other relative, who had the privilege of slaughtering them and acquiring new names—one of the greatest distinctions which a *Tupinamba* coveted. The prisoners were also traded for feathers or other ornaments. In many cases, the only outward sign of the prisoner's status was a cotton rope tied around his neck, which, according to some sources, was a symbolical necklace strung with as many beads as he had months to live until his execution. The captives were in no way hampered in their movements; they knew perfectly well that there was no place to which they could escape, for their own groups, far from welcoming them, would even have killed any member who attempted to return. On the other hand, to be killed ceremonially and then eaten was the fate for which any brave longed once he had lost his liberty. Nothing would have reminded a prisoner of his impending death if, on certain occasions, he had not been exhibited in public and again exposed to jeers and provocations. At drinking bouts, portions of his body were allotted beforehand to the carousers, each of whom—in the victim's presence—learned the part he was to receive at the ceremonial execution.

The village council chose the date of execution and sent invitations to friendly communities. Preparations for the sacrifice started a long time in advance. . . . The rites observed in these cases started after the arrival of the guests and lasted 3 to 5 days. . . . The day before the execution the prisoner was given a chance to escape but was immediately pursued. The person who overtook and overpowered him in a wrestling combat adopted a new name, as did the ceremonial executioner. . . . Festivities began that night. The prisoner was often requested to dance. Apparently he did so without reluctance and took part in the general rejoicing as if he were merely a guest. He even regarded his position as enviable, for "it was an honor to die as a great warrior during dancing and drinking." . . .

The following morning the prisoner was dragged to the plaza by some old women amid cries, songs, and music. The rope was taken from his neck, passed round his waist, and held at both ends by two or more men. Again he was allowed to give vent to his feelings by throwing fruits or potsherds at his enemies. He was surrounded by women who vied in their insults. Old women, painted black and red, with necklaces of human teeth, darted out of their huts carrying newly painted vases to receive the victim's blood and entrails. A fire was lit and the ceremonial club was shown to the captive. Every man present handled the club for a while, thus acquiring the power to catch a prisoner in the future. Then the executioner appeared in full array, painted and covered with a long feather cloak. He was followed by relatives who sang and beat drums. Their bodies, like that of the executioner, were smeared with white ashes. The club was handed to the executioner by a famous old warrior, who performed a few ritual gestures with it. Then the executioner and his victim harangued each other. The executioner derided the prisoner for his imminent death, while the latter foretold the vengeance that his relatives would take and boasted of his past deeds. The captive showed despondency only if his executioner, instead of being an experienced warrior, was merely a young man who had never been on the battlefield. The execution itself was a cruel game. Enough liberty was allowed the prisoner to dodge the blows, and sometimes a club was put in his hands so that he could parry them without being able to strike. When at last he fell down, his skull shattered, everybody shouted and whistled. The position of the body was interpreted as an omen for the executioner. The prisoner's wife shed a few tears over his body and then joined in the cannibalistic banquet.

Old women rushed to drink the warm blood, and children were invited to dip their hands in it. Mothers would smear their nipples with blood so that even babies could have a taste of it. The body, cut into quarters, was roasted on a barbecue and the old women, who were the most eager for human flesh, licked the grease running along the sticks. Some portions, reputed to be delicacies or sacred, such as the fingers or the grease around the liver or heart, were allotted to distinguished guests. . . .

# 7 / PSYCHOANALYSIS AMONG THE IROQUOIS OF NEW YORK STATE

*The Iroquois were the only Indians north of Mexico who were organized into a confederacy before contact with Europeans. All other confederacies in the United States and Canada were formed after White contact as an expedient means of resisting aggression from without. From 1649 to 1684 the Iroquois ran roughshod over most of their neighbors, some of whom were almost annihilated. Although they were probably the most aggressive and war-oriented tribe in all the Americas during this period, it is clear from Wallace's sensitive article that they suffered psychological reactions to this brutal activity. Nightmares of humiliation and torture filled their dreams and haunted even their waking hours. These personal disturbances were treated most often by a sort of group psychotherapy in which the worried and frightened individual recounted his dreams in public or asked the group assembled to guess the content and meaning of his dreams. The proud and relentless warrior was thus reduced to the role of a helpless patient eager to receive help from his fellow tribesmen. The Iroquoian theory of personality in the seventeenth century was remarkably close to that of Sigmund Freud, which was developed more than two centuries later.*

This paper is essentially ethnographic; it describes the theory and practice, relative to dreams, reported by Jesuit missionaries among

Anthony F. C. Wallace, "Dreams and Wishes of the Soul: A Type of Psychoanalytic Theory among the Seventeenth Century Iroquois," *American Anthropologist*, LX (1958), 234-48.

the seventeenth-century Iroquois. However, the data raise questions of both theoretical and historical interest: for we find here a "primitive" people actively using a theory of the mind similar in many essentials to that expressed by Sigmund Freud and his intellectual heirs in Western European cultural tradition of two centuries later. It is at least an interesting case of independent invention (for I see no evidence of Iroquois dream theory having influenced Freud, directly or indirectly). . . .

The black-robed Jesuit fathers began the preaching of the gospel to the Seneca nation in the year 1668. They quickly found that the Seneca were rigidly attached to Iroquoian religious traditions and were particularly obstinate in looking to their dreams for guidance in all the important affairs of life. Father Fremin wrote:

The Iroquois have, properly speaking, only a single Divinity—the dream. To it they render their submission, and follow all its orders with the utmost exactness. The Tsonnontouens [Seneca] are more attached to this superstition than any of the others; their Religion in this respect becomes even a matter of scruple; whatever it be that they think they have done in their dreams, they believe themselves absolutely obliged to execute at the earliest moment. The other nations content themselves with observing those of their dreams which are the most important; but this people, which has the reputation of living more religiously than its neighbors, would think itself guilty of a great crime if it failed in its observance of a single dream. The people think only of that, they talk about nothing else, and all their cabins are filled with their dreams. They spare no pains, no industry, to show their attachment thereto, and their folly in this particular goes to such an excess as would be hard to imagine. He who has dreamed during the night that he was bathing, runs immediately, as soon as he rises, all naked, to several cabins, in each of which he has a kettleful of water thrown over his body, however cold the weather may be. Another who has dreamed that he was taken prisoner and burned alive, has found himself bound and burned like a captive on the next day, being persuaded that by thus satisfying his dream, this fidelity will avert from him the pain and infamy of captivity and death,—which, according to what he has learned from his Divinity, he is otherwise bound to suffer among his enemies. Some have been known to go as far as Quebec, traveling a hundred and fifty leagues, for the sake of getting a dog, that they had dreamed of buying there. . . .

The Iroquois theory of dreams was basically psychoanalytic. Father Ragueneau in 1649 described the theory in language which might have been used by Freud himself.

In addition to the desires which we generally have that are free, or at least voluntary in us, [and] which arise from a previous knowledge of some goodness that we imagine to exist in the thing desired, the Hurons [and, he might have added, the Seneca] believe that our souls have other desires, which are, as it were, inborn and concealed. These, they say, come from the depths of the soul, not through any knowledge, but by means of a certain blind transporting of the soul to certain objects; these transports might in the language of philosophy be called *Desideria innata,* to distinguish them from the former, which are called *Desideria Elicita.*

Now they believe that our soul makes these natural desires known by means of dreams, which are its language. Accordingly, when these desires are accomplished, it is satisfied; but on the contrary, if it be not granted what it desires, it becomes angry, and not only does not give its body the good and the happiness that it wished to procure for it, but often it also revolts against the body, causing various diseases, and even death. . . .

In consequence of these erroneous [thought Father Ragueneau] ideas, most of the Hurons are very careful to note their dreams, and to provide the soul with what it has pictured to them during their sleep. If, for instance, they have seen a javelin in a dream, they try to get it; if they have dreamed that they gave a feast, they will give one on awakening, if they have the wherewithal; and so on with other things. And they call this *Ondinnonk*—a secret desire of the soul manifested by a dream.

Intuitively, the Iroquois had achieved a great degree of psychological sophistication. They recognized conscious and unconscious parts of the mind. They knew the great force of unconscious desires, and were aware that the frustration of these desires could cause mental and physical ("psychosomatic") illness. They understood that these desires were expressed in symbolic form by dreams, but that the individual could not always properly interpret these dreams himself. They had noted the distinction between the manifest and latent content of dreams, and employed what sounds like the technique of free association to uncover the latent meaning. And they considered that the best method for the relief of psychic and psychosomatic distress was to give the frustrated desire satisfaction, either directly or symbolically.

The dreams reported by the Jesuit fathers, and in the ethnological literature up to the present time, provide a measure of the range and types of manifest content, and to a degree of the latent content, of Iroquois dreams. Dreams involving overt sexuality were not rare, and since they were freely reported and often acted out in therapeutic orgies, they gave the fathers great concern. Normally the Iroquoian peoples were modest in dress, often rather shy in heterosexual contacts, and although premarital affairs were freely permitted to the young people and divorce and remarriage were easy for adults, chastity and marital fidelity were publicly recognized ideals. The fulfillment of dream wishes, however, took priority over other proprieties.

In 1656, at Onondaga, three warriors came to the village during the Midwinter Ceremony. They had been absent for a year in an unsuccessful campaign against the Cat, or Erie, Nation. One of the warriors "was as wasted, pale, and depressed, as if he had spoken with the Devil. He spat blood, and was so disfigured that one scarcely dared to look him in the face." This man, when he arrived, announced that he had a matter of great importance to communicate to the elders. When they had assembled, he told them that during the campaign he had seen Tarachiawagon, He-who-holds-up-the-sky, the culture hero, in the guise of a little dwarf. Tarachiawagon had addressed the warrior thus:

> I am he who holds up the Sky, and the guardian of the earth; I preserve men, and give victories to warriors. I have made you masters of the earth and victors over so many Nations: I made you conquer the Hurons, the Tobacco Nation, the Ahondihronnons, Atiraguenrek, Atiaonrek, Takoulguehronnons and Gentaguetehronnons; in short, I have made you what you are: and if you wish me to continue my protection over you, hear my words, and execute my orders.
>
> First, you will find three Frenchmen in your village when you arrive there. Secondly, you will enter during the celebration of the Honnaouroria. Thirdly, after your arrival, let there be sacrificed to me ten dogs, ten porcelain beads from each cabin, a collar [belt of wampum] ten rows wide, four measures of sunflower seed, and as many of beans. And, as for thee, let two married women be given thee, to be at thy

disposal for five days. If that be not executed item by item I will make thy Nation a prey to all sorts of disaster,—and, after it is all done, I will declare to thee my orders for the future.

The dreamer's demands were fulfilled. . . .

During the dream guessing rites at Midwinter and, on occasion of illness, at other times of the year, persons propounded riddles in a sacred game. Each person or a group announced his "own and special desire or 'Ondinonc'—according as he is able to get information and enlightenment by dreams—not openly, however, but through Riddles. For example, someone will say, 'What I desire and what I am seeking is that which bears a lake within itself'; and by this is intended a pumpkin or calabash. Another will say, 'What I ask for is seen in my eyes—it will be marked with various colors'; and because the same Huron word that signifies 'eye' also signifies 'glass bead,' this is a clue to divine what he desires—namely, some kinds of beads of this material, and of different colors. Another will intimate that he desires an Andacwandat feast—that is to say, many fornications and adulteries. His Riddle being guessed, there is no lack of persons to satisfy his desire."

Nightmares of torture and personal loss were apparently not uncommon among warriors. In 1642 a Huron man dreamed that non-Huron Iroquois had taken him and burned him as a captive. As soon as he awoke, a council was held. "The ill fortune of such a Dream," said the chiefs, "must be averted." At once twelve or thirteen fires were lighted in the cabin where captives were burned, and torturers seized fire brands. The dreamer was burned; "he shrieked like a madman. When he avoided one fire, he at once fell into another." Naked, he stumbled around the fires three times, singed by one torch after another, while his friends repeated compassionately, "courage, my Brother, it is thus that we have pity on thee." Finally he darted out of the ring, seized a dog held for him there, and paraded through the cabins with this dog on his shoulders, publicly offering it as a consecrated victim to the demon of war, "begging him to accept this semblance instead of the reality of his Dream." The dog was finally killed with a club, roasted in the flames, and eaten at a public feast, "in the same manner as they usually eat their captives. . . ." In the period 1645-49, Father

Francesco Bressani saw a Huron cut off a finger with a sea-shell because he had dreamed that his enemies had captured him and were performing this amputation. . . . In 1661-62, Father Lalemant describes three similar cases among the Five Nations. One man, in order to satisfy the dictates of his dream, had himself stripped naked by his friends, bound, dragged through the streets with the customary hooting, set upon the scaffold, and the fires lit. "But he was content with all these preliminaries, and, after passing some hours in singing his death song, thanked the company, believing that after this imaginary captivity he would never be actually a prisoner." Another man having dreamt that his cabin was on fire, "could find no rest until he could see it actually burning." The chief's council in a body, "after mature deliberation on the matter," ceremoniously burned it down for him. A third man went to such extremes of realism, after a captivity nightmare, that he determined "that the fire should be actually applied to his legs, in the same way as to captives when their final torture is begun." The roasting was so cruel and prolonged that it took six months for him to recover from his burns.

Some dreams were violently aggressive. One Huron dreamed that he killed a French priest. "I killed a Frenchman; that is my dream. Which must be fulfilled at any cost," he yelled. He was only appeased by being given a French coat supposedly taken from the body of a dead Frenchman. A Cayuga man dreamed that he gave a feast of human flesh. He invited all the chief men of the Cayuga nation to his cabin to hear a matter of importance. "When they had assembled, he told them that he was ruined, as he had had a dream impossible of fulfillment; that his ruin would entail that of the whole Nation; and that a universal overthrow and destruction of the earth was to be expected. He enlarged at great length on the subject, and then asked them to guess his dream. All struck wide of the mark, until one man, suspecting the truth, said to him: 'Thou wishest to give a feast of human flesh. Here, take my brother; I place him in thy hands to be cut up on the spot, and put into the kettle.' All present were seized with fright, except the dreamer, who said that his dream required a woman." A young girl was adorned with ornaments and, unaware of her fate, led to the dreamer-executioner. "He took her; they watched his actions, and pitied that innocent girl; but, when they thought him about to deal the death-blow, he cried out: 'I am satisfied; my dream requires nothing further.' . . ." During the "Feast of Fools," the annual *Ononharoia* or "turning the brain upside down," when men and women ran madly from cabin to cabin, acting out their dreams in charades and demanding the dream be guessed and satisfied, many women and men alike dreamt of fighting natural enemies. Dreams in which hostility was directed at members of other nations were properly satisfied by acting them out both in pantomime and in real life; but bad dreams about members of the same community were acted out only in some symbolic form, which had a prophylactic effect. Thus, someone on the Cornplanter Seneca Reservation (during the nineteenth century) dreamed that a certain young woman was alone in a canoe, in the middle of a stream, without a paddle. The dreamer invited the young lady to a dream-guessing ceremony at his home. Various people gathered and each one tried to guess what the dream was. Finally the dream was guessed. A miniature canoe with a paddle was thereupon presented to the girl. This ceremony was expected to forestall the dream disaster from happening in real life. . . .

Dreams were very common in which the dreamer met a super-natural being who promised to be a friend and patron and to give his protégé special powers and responsibilities. They were often experienced by boys at puberty who deliberately sought such guardian spirits. . . .

Dreams of supernatural protectors (or persecutors) also came often to sick persons, and the appropriate therapeutic ritual was deduced from the identity of the spirit. Thus, dreams of false-faces call for the curing rituals of the Society of Faces; dreams of birds (in recent years, particularly of bloody or headless chickens) indi-cated that the Dew Eagle Ceremony was required. Sick persons often dreamed of someone (or a relative of the sick person dreamed), and the dream was interpreted to mean that the sick person "wants a friend." During the Eagle Society Ceremony, the sick person is given a "ceremonial friend"; thereafter the two treat one another as kin-folk, and the relationship of mutual helpfulness is life-long. . . .

The force of the unconscious desires of the individual, which are so compelling that "it would be cruelty, nay, murder, not to give a man the subject of his dream; for such a refusal might cause his death," sometimes was reinforced by the fact that in native theory they were the vehicle for expressing the desires and commands of the supernatural beings whom his wandering dreamsoul had met. Some of these supernatural dreams have already been mentioned. Those involving powerful supernaturals like Tarachiawagon were apt to achieve a great notoriety, and (if the chiefs considered the dream ominous) the whole nation might exert itself to fulfill the dreamer's demands; neglect invited national disaster. In the winter of 1640, during an epidemic of smallpox among the Huron, a young fisherman had a vision: a demon appeared to him under the form of a tall and handsome young man. "Fear not," said the being, "I am the master of the earth, whom you Hurons honor under the name of Iouskeha. I am the one whom the French wrongly call Jesus, but they do not know me. I have pity on your country, which I have taken under my protection; I come to teach you both the reasons and the remedies for your misfortune. It is the strangers who alone are the cause of it; they now travel two by two through the country, with the design of spreading the disease everywhere. They will not stop with that; after this smallpox which now depopulates your cabins, there will follow certain colics which in less than three days will carry off all those whom this disease may not have removed. You can prevent this misfortune; drive out from your village the two black gowns who are there." The demon continued with prescriptions for distributing medicinal waters to the sick, but after a few days, apparently, the popular disturbance subsided and the priests were not expelled. . . .

In Iroquois theory, a dream could thus reveal the wishes not only of the dreamer but also of the supernatural who appeared in his dream. Frustration of the wishes of a supernatural was dangerous, for he might not merely abandon or cause the death of the dreamer, but bring about disaster to the whole society or even cause the end of the world. Hence, dreams in which such powerful personages as Tarachiawagon (culture hero and a favorite dream-figure) appeared and announced that they wanted something done (frequently for the dreamer) were matters of national moment. Clairvoyants were called upon; the chiefs met, and discussed ways of satisfying the sometimes expensive or awkward demands of the dreamers (representing the powers above), or of averting the predicted catastrophe. Not infrequently this type of dream also bore elements of personality transformation for the dreamer, who in his identification with the gods assumed a new role as prophet, messiah, and public censor and adviser. Such prophets might make detailed recommendations about the storage of crops, the waging of war, diplomatic policy toward other tribes and toward the French or the English, measures to avert epidemics or famine. Rarely, however, did such prophets maintain a lasting influence.

The theory of dreams among the Iroquois is in evident accord with the theme of freedom in the culture as a whole. The intolerance of externally imposed restraints, the principle of individual independence and autonomy, the maintenance of an air of indifference to pain, hardship, and loneliness—all these are the negative expression, as it were, of the positive assertion that wishes must be satisfied, that frustration of desire is the root of all evil. But men are never equally aware and equally tolerant of all their desires; and dreams themselves, carefully examined, are perhaps the quickest portal to that shadowy region where the masked and banished wishes exist in limbo. What, if anything, can we learn about the unconscious of Iroquois Indians from the scattered dreams recorded by the Jesuits and other casual observers?

The manifest content of Iroquois dreams is probably as various as the wishes of mankind: there are dreams of love and hate, pleasure and pain, of lost loved ones and longed-for guardians; inconsequential and absurd things happen, and trivial objects are transfixed by the arrow of desire; abhorrent actions and repulsive thoughts plague the restless sleeper. Dreams as reported in the literature seem to have held a prevailingly anxious tone, ranging from nightmare fantasies of torture to the nagging need to define the unconscious wish and satisfy it before some disaster occurs. The most dramatic and most frequently mentioned dreams seem to come from three groups of people: pubescent youths (who must renounce childhood's indulgences); warriors (who fear capture and torture); and the sick (who fear to die). These are perhaps the stress points which generate desire. Adolescent conflict, dreams of battle, and the silent panic of the sick: these are things of which men of many cultures, including our own, have experience.

The manifest content, and the conscious rationale the Seneca themselves give to dreams, are largely in active voice; such passivity as shows itself is laden with pain, unless it occurs in transformation dreams, where a man may be passive in relation to a god. But the latent content, representative of the underlying wish, may be seen in the acting out which is so often passive or self-destructive. Dreams are not to brood over, to analyze, and to prompt lonely and independent action; they are to be told, or at least hinted at, and it is for other people to be active. The community rallies round the dreamer with gifts and ritual. The dreamer is fed; he is danced over; he is rubbed with ashes; he is sung to; he is given valuable presents; he is accepted as a member of a medicine society. A man whose dream manifests a wish to attack and kill is satisfied by being given a coat, a man who dreams of sleeping with a woman does not attempt to woo his mistress, he is given an available female by the chief's council. Only in the personality-transformation dreams of pubescent boys and adult prophets is passivity accepted in the dream; and these are the dreams of men in extremis.

This observation suggests that the typical Iroquois male, who in his daily life was a brave, generous, active, and independent spirit, nevertheless cherished some strong, if unconscious, wishes to be passive, to beg, to be cared for. This unallowable passive tendency, so threatening to a man's sense of self-esteem, could not appear easily even in a dream; when it did, it was either experienced as an intolerably painful episode of torture, or was put in terms of a meeting with a supernatural protector. However, the Iroquois themselves unwittingly make the translation: an active manifest dream is fulfilled by a passive, receiving action. The arrangement of the dream guessing rite raises this dependency to an exquisite degree: the dreamer cannot even ask for his wish; like a baby, he must content himself with cryptic signs and symbols until someone guesses what he wants and gives it to him.

The culture of dreams may be regarded as a useful escape-valve in Iroquois life. In their daily affairs, Iroquois men were brave, active, self-reliant, and autonomous; they cringed to no one and begged for nothing. But no man can balance forever on such a pinnacle of masculinity, where asking and being given are unknown. Iroquois men dreamt; and, without shame, they received the fruits of their dreams and their souls were satisfied.

# 8 / THE SELF-EFFACING ZUÑI OF NEW MEXICO

*The Zuñi were probably the occupants of the "seven cities of Cibola" visited briefly by Coronado in 1540. These "cities" turned out to be mere villages of a few hundred inhabitants each, and the Spanish colonists of the seventeenth century technically conquered and combined them into a single town. At this time the Spanish reported about a hundred such villages and towns, all in New Mexico except those of the Hopi in adjacent Arizona. They ranged in population from a few hundred persons to about twenty-five hundred at Pecos, near the Rio Grande River. The Spanish called these villages and towns "pueblos" and today we call the people who inhabit them Pueblo Indians, sometimes shortened to Pueblos. These people have lived in permanent settlements for more than a thousand years, subsisting principally on cultivated crops, such as maize. Compared with other Indians in the Southwest they are more peaceful, thrifty, modest in manner, and emotionally restrained.*

*Although the Zuñi came under Spanish political domination in the seventeenth century, their way of life in other respects changed little up to the beginning of the twentieth century. Ruth Bunzel, the author of this selection, lived in the town of Zuñi in the 1920's and obtained primary word-of-mouth information from a number of old Indian informants at that time. In addition, she read all the previously published reports on the Zuñi and collated them with her own data to form the sketch of their pre-Spanish life given*

Ruth L. Bunzel, "Introduction to Zuñi Ceremonialism," Bureau of American Ethnology Annual Report No. 47 (1932), pp. 474-87. (A few pronunciation marks in Zuñi words have been omitted for typographical reasons.)

*below. This appeared two years earlier than Ruth Benedict's Pat-*
*terns of Culture, and a comparison of the two publications clearly*
*shows that some of Benedict's well-phrased characterizations of the*
*Zuñi people were derived directly from Bunzel's earlier work. Bene-*
*dict acknowledges as much when she says in the preface of her work,*
*"I owe a great debt to Dr. Ruth L. Bunzel, who learned the Zuñi*
*language and whose accounts of Zuñi and collections of texts are the*
*best of all the available pueblo studies."*

The Zuñis have been agriculturists for many centuries. Since very
early prehistoric time they have raised maize, beans, and squash by
a system of dry cultivation. From the first Spanish settlers they
obtained the seeds of wheat. This, however, could be grown only
in specially favored localities which could be irrigated by hand from
large, permanently flowing springs. Recently, in 1909, the waters
of one fork of the Zuñi River have been impounded behind a dam
built by the United States Government. From this reservoir sufficient water is drawn to irrigate a strip of land on the north bank of
the river immediately adjacent to the village. This strip, approximately 1 mile wide and 6 miles long, is well suited for the cultivation of wheat and alfalfa. Maize is still raised by old methods of dry
farming on sandy fields lying at a considerable distance from the
village, mainly situated on the south bank.

From the Spaniards, also, the Zuñis got their first sheep. They
now own large and profitable herds. These are kept in remote parts
of the reservation. The wealthiest herders even rent land in surrounding townships. Rabbits are still hunted, primarily for sport,
but the deer and antelope, once important items in Zuñi economy,
have vanished from the mountains. Sheep, furthermore, are the
chief source of negotiable wealth. The sale of wool in June and of
lambs in October provides the herders with a considerable cash
income for the purchase of luxuries of white manufacture. They
have, also, horses derived from the same source and a few cattle,
but the land is not suitable for cattle breeding. Cattle are not
milked and are used for meat only. Some women have a few pigs
and chickens. The labor of agriculture and herding is done entirely
by the men. . . .

The 1,900 inhabitants live, for the most part, in Zuñi proper and
its immediate vicinity. There are, however, three large farming

villages and one small one, which are occupied for varying periods during the summer months. Even those families that make their homes there permanently return to Zuñi after harvest time for the period of the great ceremonies in December and January. . . .

Despite modern expansion the main village still remains a unit whose physical compactness is reflected in an intricate and closely knit social organization.

There are households, kinship groups, clans, tribal and special secret societies, and cult groups. A man must belong to several of these groups, and the number to which he may potentially belong is almost unlimited. There is no exclusive membership. He is born into a certain household, and his kinship and clan affiliations are thus fixed, unless altered by adoption. At puberty he is initiated into one of the six dance groups that comprise the male tribal society. He may, through sickness, be conscripted into one of the medicine societies; if he takes a scalp he must join the warriors society; and if connected with a sacerdotal household he may be called upon to join one of the priesthoods.

These groups all have their joint activities and a great part of a man's time is spent in participation in these activities. His economic activities are all bound up with the household, a communal unit to which he has certain obligations. His ordinary social contacts are all predetermined by his family and clan affiliations. Religious participation is confined to attendance at the ceremonies of those groups with which he is identified. In fact, the only sphere in which he acts as an individual rather than as a member of a group is that of sex. A man's courtship and marriage are matters of individual choice. In the bid for attention they suffer from being entirely divorced from group activity. At Zuñi no action that is entirely personal and individual receives more than passing interest. Births, deaths, and initiations figure largely in local gossip—marriages do not. It is curious to note that among the culturally related Hopi, where a marriage is the occasion for elaborate gift exchanges between the clans of the bride and groom, weddings are one of the most frequent topics of conversation.

The economic unit is the household, whose nature and methods of function illustrate admirably certain very fundamental Zuñi attitudes. The household is a group of variable composition, consisting theoretically of a maternal family; that is, a woman and her husband, her daughters with their husbands and children. To this permanent population is added a fluctuating group of miscellaneous male relatives of the maternal line—the unmarried, widowed, divorced, and those rendered homeless by passing domestic storms. This group occupies a single house consisting of several connecting rooms. There is a single kitchen drawing upon a common storehouse. The household owns certain cultivated fields which can not be alienated. In addition, the various male members individually own certain fields—generally fields recently brought under cultivation—which remain their own after they have severed connection with the household. However, all fields, whether collectively or individually owned, are cultivated by the cooperative labor of the entire male population of the household. The products go into the common storeroom to become the collective property of the women of the household. The women draw on the common stores for daily food and trade the surplus for other commodities. Sheep are owned individually by men but are herded cooperatively by groups of male kindred. When the profits of the shearing are divided a man is expected out of these to provide clothing for himself, his wife and children, including children by previous marriages, and his mother and unmarried sisters, in case they are not otherwise provided for.

Personal relations within the household are characterized by the same lack of individual authority and responsibility that marks the economic arrangements. The household has no authoritative head to enforce any kind of discipline. There is no final arbiter in disputes; no open conflict. Ordinarily the female contingent of blood relatives presents a united front. A man finding himself out of harmony with the group may withdraw quietly whenever he chooses and ally himself with another group. With his departure obligations cease, and his successor fathers his children. Diffusion of authority and responsibility is especially marked in the treatment of children.

The tribe is divided into 13 matrilineal exogamous clans, varying greatly in size from the Yellowwood, consisting of two male members, and which will therefore become extinct with the present generation, to the large so-called Dogwood (Pi'tcikwe) clan, which comprises several hundreds of individuals. . . . There is some indication of a joking relationship between a man and women of his father's clan, especially his father's blood sister, who is also his most important ceremonial relative. A woman has important ceremonial obligations to her brother's children, especially his male children, and in most cases she is compensated for her services. The clan as such has no social or political functions, although each individual feels his closest ties to be with members of his clan, upon whom he calls for assistance in any large enterprise, such as harvest, housebuilding, initiations, etc. His closest ties, naturally, are with blood kin, especially the maternal household in which he was born.

Each male is initiated at puberty into the katcina or mask dance society, which thereby assumes the rôle of a tribal cult, in distinction to other ceremonial groups of more restricted membership. Other ceremonial groups are the 12 medicine societies composed of medicine men and those whom they have cured, the war society, the rain priesthoods, and innumerable minor cults, consisting in the main of members of maternal households to whom are intrusted the care of various objects of fetishistic power. Most men of advanced age are affiliated with several of these groups.

The real political authority of the tribe is vested in the council of priests, consisting of three members of the chief priesthood and the heads of the three other priesthoods. The head of the hierarchy is the head of the chief priesthood—the house chief . . . , who is priest of the sun and keeper of the calendar, is, as his name indicates, a sort of talking chief for the priesthood. Two bow priests, members of the war society, act as messengers and the executive arm of the priesthood. The heads of the katcina society are called on in an advisory capacity in matters relating to their province. The principal matters to come before the council for decision are the appointment of civil officers, choice of the impersonators of the gods at the annual festival, the insertion of important ceremonies, such as the tribal initiation, into the regular calendar, the discussion of what action should be taken in cases of calamity, such as earthquakes and drought, the determination of tribal policy in new contingencies— such questions as whether automobiles are fire, and should therefore be taboo during the winter solstice. The maintenance of these policies is the duty of the bow priests and the secular officers.

The priests [except for the bow priests] do not act in secular affairs, being too sacred to contaminate themselves with dispute or wrangling. Crime and warfare are the concerns of the bow priests. Civil law and relations with aliens, especially the United States Government, are delegated to the secular officers appointed by the council.

The only crime that is recognized is witchcraft. An accusation of having caused death by sorcery may be brought by the relatives of the deceased. The bow priests examine the accused and review the evidence. If found guilty in former days the accused was hung by his wrists and subjected to other forms of torture until he confessed. If the confession was of such a nature as to vitiate his power by revealing its source, a common Zuñi idea, he might be released at the discretion of the bow priests, or he might be executed. Public torture and execution of witches has been stopped by Government authorities but convicted witches may be done away with secretly unless they escape to other villages.

Revelation of the secrets of the katcina cult to the uninitiated is a crime against the gods and is punishable by death by decapitation. Punishment is meted out by masked impersonators of the gods, appointed by the heads of the katcina society. No such executions have taken place within the memory of living men, but they figure prominently in folklore, and the authority and readiness of the priests so to act is never questioned in Zuñi. Flogging by masked impersonators has recently been substituted for execution. During one of the writer's visits katcinas were summoned to administer punishment to a youth found guilty of selling a mask. The accused escaped so the katcinas whipped all men in the kivas for purification.

Crimes of personal violence are rare, but such as do occur are considered matters for private adjustment, either with or without the help of the civil officers. Murder by overt means, not sorcery, bodily injury, rape, and theft are settled by property payments by the family of the guilty man to the family of the one who has been wronged. These payments are made promptly and quietly by the guilty man's relatives, since they are likely to fare worse in the hands of the officers than in those of private individuals. Adultery is not a crime. Along with stinginess and ill temper it is a frequent source of domestic infelicity and divorce, but is never regarded as a violation of rights. Sexual jealousy is no justification for violence.

The chief duties of the [civil] officers (governor, lieutenant governor, and eight tenientes) are the adjudication of civil suits, such as boundaries, water rights, inheritance, restitution for loss or injury to livestock, management of cooperative enterprises of a nonreligious character, such as road building, cleaning of irrigation ditches, execution of Government ordinances regarding registration, schooling, etc., and all manner of negotiation with outside powers. Because of the increasingly diversified contacts with whites, the office of governor is becoming more and more exacting and influential, although it still lacks prestige in native opinion. The civil officers hold office at the pleasure of the priests and may be removed by them at any time and for any cause. The office is not one that is sought, since the settlement of disputes must inevitably be a source of grievance to someone, and the thing that a Zuñi will avoid above anything else is giving offense.

In all social relations, whether within the family group or outside, the most honored personality traits are a pleasing address, a yielding disposition, and a generous heart. All the sterner virtues—initiative, ambition, an uncompromising sense of honor and justice, intense personal loyalties—not only are not admired but are heartily deplored. The woman who cleaves to her husband through misfortune and family quarrels, the man who speaks his mind where flattery would be much more comfortable, the man, above all, who thirsts for power or knowledge, who wishes to be, as they scornfully phrase it, "a leader of his people," receives nothing but censure and will very likely be persecuted for sorcery.

A characterization intended to convey the highest praise was the following: "Yes, —— is a nice polite man. No one ever hears anything from him. He never gets into trouble. He's Badger clan and Muhekwe kiva and he always dances in the summer dances." The informant could be eloquent enough when she wished to detract.

No single fact gives a better index to Zuñi temperament than that suicide is absolutely unknown among them, and the very idea is so remote from their habits of thought that it arouses only laughter.

In so far as the culture of any people is an integrated and harmonious whole, it shows in all its phases the same character and individuality. At Zuñi the same ceremonious collectivism that characterizes social activities is the essence also of all religious participation. The relation between man and the supernatural is as free of tragic intensity as the relation of man to man. The supernatural, conceived always as a collectivity, a multiple manifestation of the divine essence, is approached by the collective force of the people in a series of great public and esoteric rituals whose richness, variety, and beauty have attracted the attention of poets and artists of all countries. Nowhere in the New World, except in the ancient civilizations of Mexico and Yucatan, has ceremonialism been more highly developed, and nowhere, including these civilizations, has it gone so far toward taming man's frenzy. In Zuñi, as in all the pueblos, religion spreads wide. It pervades all activities, and its very pervasiveness and the rich and harmonious forms in which it is externalized compensate the student of religion for the lack of intensity of that feeling. For although the Zuñi may be called one of the most thoroughly religious peoples of the world, in all the enormous mass of rituals there is no single bit of religious feeling equal in intensity and exaltation to the usual vision quest of the North American Indian.

According to Zuñi belief, man has a spiritual substance, a soul (tse'makwin, thoughts, from tse'ma, to think, ponder). This is associated with the head, the heart, and the breath. The head is the seat of skill and intelligence, but the heart is the seat of the emotions and of profound thought. "I shall take it to my heart" means I shall ponder it carefully, and remember it long. The word for life is tekohanane, literally daylight. The breath is the symbol of life. It also is the means by which spiritual substances communicate and the seat of [impersonal] power or mana. Inhaling is an act of ritual blessing. One inhales from all sacred objects to derive benefit from their mana. At the end of any prayer or chant all present inhale; holding their folded hand before their nostrils, in order to partake of the sacred essence of prayer. The feather is the pictorial representation of the breath. Death occurs when "the heart wears out." When a person is very sick his heart is wearing out. "Medicine men can fix it up when they come to cure, and it will go for a while, but sooner or later you will have to get a new one." Getting a new heart is the first rite in society initiations.

Dreams are believed to be of supernatural causation, and foretell the future if one can properly interpret them. Certain persons in particular are believed to "dream true." Dreams of the dead are believed to be visitations of the dead, and are always portents of death. Visual and auditory hallucinations are believed to be similarly caused. "Bad dreams," a term which includes hallucinations, is a disease of supernatural origin, as opposed to bodily disease, which is caused by witchcraft. There are special rituals for curing "bad dreams," to which we shall allude frequently in the following pages.

In rare instances the soul can leave the body and return to it again. This occurs during sickness and is a matter of great seriousness. A friend has reported such an experience as follows:

"When I was sick of the measles I was very sick. On the third day I didn't know anything. Maybe I fainted or maybe I really died and came back. I never believed that could happen, but it really did, because when I came back the room was going round and round and there was a little light coming through the window, although there was a bright light in the room. While I was dead I dreamed I was going toward the west." The narrative goes on to describe her encounter with her dead grandfather and unknown dead women, her "aunts."

"I was so happy to see my grandfather. Since then I've never worried about dying, even when I was very sick, because I saw all these dead people and saw that they were still living the way we do." After this experience the girl was initiated into a medicine society, to "save her life," because her people (i.e., the dead) had asked her for feathers.

Visual and auditory hallucinations are caused by supernaturals. They are regarded as omens of death. The most common hallucinations of this type are the apparent movement of sacred objects on an altar—especially masks.

Death is usually caused by witchcraft. The usual method of the sorcerer is to shoot foreign bodies into his victim. But other more indirect methods may be used. Sorcery, however, is never practiced openly as in Oceania. No one admits having sorcery, and everyone suspects others very vaguely. Suspicion of sorcery subjects a person to social ostracism, but a death caused by sorcery is an occasion for formal interference on the part of the [Indian legal] authorities. There is considerable internal and comparative evidence in the body of witchcraft belief and practice to indicate that their present great development is post-Hispanic, and that the belief in less specific supernatural causation is earlier and more aboriginal.

Considerable confusion exists in the Zuñi mind concerning the fate of the soul after death. General folk belief has it that for four days after death it remains in Zuñi, causing great inconvenience, and, indeed, danger, to survivors, and on the fourth day departs for Katcina Village (koluwalawa) in the west. . . .

To the Zuñi the whole world appears animate. Not only are night and day, wind, clouds, and trees possessed of personality, but even articles of human manufacture, such as houses, pots, and clothing, are alive and sentient. All matter has its inseparable spiritual essence. For the most part this spiritual aspect of things is vague and impersonal. Although all objects are called ho'i, "living person," in a figurative sense, they are not definitely anthropomorphic; they have consciousness but they do not possess human faculties. To all these beings is applied the term kapin ho'i, "raw person"; man, on the other hand, is a "cooked" person.

Prayers are full of description of natural phenomena in anthropomorphic guise. I quote some of the most striking.

When our sun father
Goes in to sit down at his ancient place,
And our night fathers,
Our mothers,
Night priests,
Raise their dark curtain over their ancient place. . . .

That our earth mother may wrap herself
In a fourfold robe of white meal;
That she may be covered with frost flowers;
That yonder on all the mossy mountains,
The forests may huddle together with the cold;
That their arms may be broken by the snow,
In order that the land may be thus,
I have made my prayer sticks into living beings.

Following wherever the roads of the rain makers come out,
May the ice blanket spread out,
May the ice blanket cover the country;
All over the land

May the flesh of our earth mother
Crack open from the cold;
That your thoughts may bend to this,
That your words may be to this end;
For this with prayers I send you forth.

When our earth mother is replete with living waters,
When spring comes,
The source of our flesh
All the different kinds of corn,
We shall lay to rest in the ground,
With their earth mother's living waters.
They will be made into new beings.
Coming out standing into the daylight
Of their sun father,
Calling for rain,
To all sides they will stretch out their hands.
Then from wherever the rain makers stay quietly
They will send forth their misty breath;
Their massed clouds filled with water will come out to sit down with us;
Far from their homes,
With outstretched hands of water they will embrace the corn,
Stepping down to caress them with their fresh waters,
With their fine rain caressing the earth,
With their heavy rain caressing the earth,
And yonder, wherever the roads of the rain makers come forth,
Torrents will rush forth,
Silt will rush forth,
Mountains will be washed out,
Logs will be washed down,
Yonder all the mossy mountains
Will drip with water.
The clay-lined hollows of our earth mother
Will overflow with water,
From all the lakes
Will rise the cries of the children of the rain makers,
In all the lakes
There will be joyous dancing—
Desiring that it should be thus,
I send forth my prayers.

That our earth mother
May wear a fourfold green robe,

Full of moss,
Full of flowers,
Full of pollen,
That the land may be thus
I have made you into living beings.
That yonder in all our water-filled fields
The source of our flesh,
All the different kinds of corn
May stand up all about,
That, nourishing themselves with fresh water,
Clasping their children in their arms,
They may rear their young,
So that we may bring them into our houses,
Thinking of them toward whom our thoughts bend—
Desiring this,
I send you forth with prayers. . . .

Of this animate universe man is an integral part. The beings about him are neither friendly nor hostile. In so far as all are harmonious parts of the whole, the surrounding forces sustain and preserve humanity in the status quo.

Among these vague impersonal forces are certain clearly defined individuals and classes of beings who definitely influence human affairs. These are such beings as the sun, the earth, the corn, prey animals, and the gods of war. These are called a'wonawi'lona "the ones who hold our roads." They, too, belong to man's world, and have no animus against man. But in as much as they may withhold their gifts, their assistance must be secured by offerings, prayers, and magical practices.

The sense of conflict as the basic principle of life does not dominate man's relation to the universe any more than it dominates man's relation to man. The Promethean theme—man's tragic and heroic struggle against the gods—has no place in Zuñi philosophic speculation. Nor have any of the other concepts of cosmic conflicts which have always absorbed the interest of Asiatic and European philosophers and mystics, the antithesis between good and evil, or between matter and spirit. There is no Satan in Zuñi ideology, and no Christ.

The world, then, is as it is, and man's plan in it is what it is. Day follows night and the cycles of the years complete themselves. In the spring the corn is planted, and if all goes well the young stalks grow to maturity and fulfill themselves. They are cut down to serve man for food, but their seeds remain against another planting. So man, too, has his days and his destined place in life. His road may be long or short, but in time it is fulfilled and he passes on to fill another rôle in the cosmic scheme. He, too, leaves his seed behind him. Man dies but mankind remains. This is the way of life; the whole literature of prayer shows no questioning of these fundamental premises. This is not resignation, the subordination of desire to a stronger force, but the sense of man's oneness with the universe. The conditions controlling human affairs are no more moral issues than those, like the blueness of the sky, to which we may well be indifferent. It is a remarkably realistic view of the universe. It is an attitude singularly free from terror, guilt, and mystery. The Zuñi feels great awe of the supernatural, and definitely fears certain beings in his pantheon—the recently dead, the Koyemci, certain "dangerous" katcinas, but this is quite different from the cosmic terror that crushes many primitive and civilized peoples.

# III / ADVANCED FARMING CULTURES

## 9 / THE BENEVOLENT DESPOTISM OF THE INCAS OF PERU

*The most distinctive achievement of the Incas of Peru was their political organization. The Inca Empire, extending for a distance of twenty-five hundred miles from Ecuador to central Chile, was not only much larger than the territory overrun by the Aztecs, but had a much more centralized government. The Incas attempted to assimilate the peoples they conquered, and the local officials who made up the lower nobility (curacas) were drawn largely from the leaders of the defeated tribes. Although the Incas required complete subservience to their emperor and his deputies in the provinces, they allowed a conquered people to retain its local gods, as well as its local officials. They superimposed their own sun-god and imperial officials on the subjugated peoples without completely suppressing their pre-Inca way of life.*

*Cieza de León participated in a number of military campaigns in Colombia and Ecuador from 1535 to 1547, and from 1547 to 1550 he devoted his full time to interviewing many Inca informants in Peru and to writing his description of Inca culture as it was before the arrival of the Spanish. He traveled extensively in Peru and combined his own direct observations in many provinces of the empire with what he learned from others. His account is generally regarded as the most authentic and reliable one from the sixteenth century. William H. Prescott mistakenly attributed the authorship*

Pedro Cieza de Léon, *The Second Part of the Chronicle of Peru*, translated and edited with notes and introduction by Clements R. Markham (London: The Hakluyt Society, 1883), pp. 26-30, 33-38, 42-62, 64-65, 67-71.

*of the second part of Cieza de León's chronicle, from which this selection is drawn, to Don Juan Sarmiento.*

And it was ordained by them that he who became king should take his sister, being the legitimate daughter of his father and mother, as his wife; in order that the succession of the kingdom might by that means be confirmed in the royal house. It appeared to them that by this means, even if such a woman, being sister of the king, should not be chaste, and should have intercourse with another man, the son thus born would still be hers, and not the son of a strange woman. They also considered that if the Inca married a strange woman, she might do the same and conceive in adultery, in such a way that, it not being known, the child would be received as a natural born son of the lord. For these reasons, and because it seemed desirable to those who ordained the laws, it was a rule among the Incas that he amongst them all who became emperor should take his sister to wife. . . . If by chance he who became lord had no sister, it was permitted that he should marry the most illustrious lady there was, and she was held to be the principal among all his women. For none of these lords had less than 700 women for the service of their house and for their pleasure. So that they all had many children by these women, who were well treated, and respected by the people. . . .

I understood, when I was in Cuzco, that it was the custom among the kings Incas, that the king, as soon as he died should be mourned for with much lamentation, and that great sacrifices should be offered up in accordance with their religion. When these ceremonies were over, the oldest people of the country discussed the life and acts of the recently deceased king, considering whether he had done good to the country, and what battles he had gained over the country's enemies. Having settled these questions, and others which we do not entirely understand, they decided whether the deceased king had been so fortunate as to merit praise and fame, and to deserve that his memory should for ever be preserved. They then called for the great *quiposcamayos* who preserve the records, and understand how to give an account of the events that occur in the kingdom. Next they communicated with those who were most expert, and who were selected for their skill in rhetoric and the use of words. These knew how to narrate the events in regular order, like ballad singers and romance writers. These compose the songs, so that they shall be heard by all at marriage ceremonies and other festivities. Thus they were instructed what to say concerning the deceased lord, and, if they treated of wars, they sang, in proper order, of the many battles he had fought in different parts of the empire. And for other events, there were songs and romances to celebrate them on suitable occasions, so that the people might be animated by the recital of what had passed in other times.

Those Indians who, by order of the kings, had learnt the romances, were honoured and favoured, and great care was taken to teach their sons and other men in their provinces who were most able and intelligent. By this plan, from the mouths of one generation the succeeding one was taught, and they can relate what took place 500 years ago, as if only ten years had passed. . . .

The memory of those who were great and good was so venerated that the successor of such an one sought no inheritance from him, but he succeeded to the empire alone. It was the law that the riches and the royal insignia of one who had been King of Cuzco should never pass to another, and should never be forgotten. . . . All the treasure which the deceased lord possessed was left in the care of his servants and confidential attendants, who brought it out at the festivals, with great ceremony. Besides this, the servants and attendants had their *chacaras*, which is their name for fields where they cultivate maize and other crops, and with these the women and family of the deceased lord were maintained, although he was dead and gone. No doubt this custom explains the fact that, in this empire, there was such vast treasure as we here beheld with our eyes. . . .

They had another method of knowing and understanding what had been received from the contributions in the provinces, what provisions were stored on the routes that the king would take with his army or when he was visiting the provinces, how much was in each place of deposit, how much was delivered out. And this method exceeded in artifice the *carastes* used by the Mexicans for their calculations. The system of the Peruvians was by *quipus*. These were long ropes made of knotted cords, and those who were accountants and understood the arrangement of these knots, could, by their means, give an account of the expenditure, and of other things during a long course of years. On these knots they counted from one to ten, and from ten to a hundred, and from a hundred to a thousand. On one of the ropes are the units, on another the tens, and so on. Each ruler of a province was provided with accountants who were called *quipucamayos,* and by these knots they kept account of what tribute was to be paid in the district, with respect to silver, gold, cloth, flocks, down to fire-wood and other minute details. By the same *quipus* they could report to those who were commissioned to take the account at the end of a year, or of ten or twenty years, with such accuracy that so much as a pair of *alpargatas* [shoes] would not be missing. . . .

There is another thing that should be known, for I take it to be very certain. The long wars, cruelties, robberies, and tyrannical treatment which these people have suffered from the Spaniards would have led to their complete destruction, if it had not been for the excellent order and concert of their regulations. But they, having been trained in the intelligent system of accounts which was established by their wise princes, made an agreement among themselves that if an army of Spaniards passed through any of the provinces, and did such damage as would be caused by the destruction of growing crops, sacking of houses, and other mischief of still worse kinds, all the accountants should make the best provision possible in the districts through which our people passed, in order that all might not be devastated. So it was arranged, and as soon as the Spaniards were gone, the chiefs assembled, the *quipus* were examined and checked, and if one province had lost more than another, that which had suffered less made up the difference: so that the burden was shared equally by all. . . .

It should be well understood that great prudence was needed to enable these kings to govern such large provinces, extending over so vast a region, parts of it rugged and covered with forests, parts mountainous, with snowy peaks and ridges, parts consisting of deserts of sand, dry and without trees or water. These regions were inhabited by many different nations, with varying languages, laws, and religions, and the kings had to maintain tranquillity and to rule so that all should live in peace and in friendship towards their lord. Although the city of Cuzco was the head of the empire, as we have remarked in many places, yet at certain points, as we shall also explain, the king stationed his delegates and governors, who were the most learned, the ablest, and the bravest men that could be found, and none was so youthful that he was not already in the last third part of his age. As they were faithful and none betrayed their trusts, and as they had the *mitimaes* [colonists] on their side, none of the natives, though they might be more powerful, attempted to rise in rebellion; or if such a thing ever did take place, the town where the revolt broke out was punished, and the ringleaders were sent prisoners to Cuzco.

Thus the kings were so feared that, when they travelled over the provinces, and permitted a piece of the cloth to be raised which hung round their litter, so as to allow their vassals to behold them, there was such an outcry that the birds fell from the upper air where they were flying, insomuch that they could be caught in men's hands. All men so feared the king, that they did not dare to speak evil even of his shadow. And this was not all. If any of the king's captains or servants went forth to visit a distant part of the empire on some business, the people came out on the road with presents to receive them, not daring, even if one came alone, to omit to comply with all his commands.

So great was the veneration that the people felt for their princes, throughout this vast region, that every district was as well regulated and governed as if the lord was actually present to chastise those who acted contrary to his rules. This fear arose from the known valour of the lords and their strict justice. It was felt to be certain that those who did evil would receive punishment without fail, and that neither prayers nor bribes would avert it. At the same time, the Incas always did good to those who were under their sway, and would not allow them to be ill-treated, nor that too much tribute should be exacted from them. Many who dwelt in a sterile country where they and their ancestors had lived with difficulty, found that through the orders of the Ynca their lands were made fertile and abundant, the things being supplied which before were wanting. In other districts, where there was scarcity of clothing, owing to the people having no flocks, orders were given that cloth should be abundantly provided. In short, it will be understood that as these lords knew how to enforce service and the payment of tribute, so they provided for the maintenance of the people, and took care that they should want for nothing. Through these good works, and because the lord always gave women and rich gifts to his principal vassals, he gained so much on their affections that he was most fondly loved. I remember having seen old Indians with my own eyes, when I was in sight of Cuzco, who gazed at the city and raised a great shout, followed by tears of sorrow at the contemplation of the present state of things, and the thought of what was passed, when for so many years they had lords in that city, of their own people, who knew how to receive their service and friendship after another fashion than that of the Spaniards. . . .

One of the things which I admired most, in contemplating and noting down the affairs of this kingdom, was to think how and in what manner they can have made such grand and admirable roads as we now see, and what a number of men would suffice for their construction, and with what tools and instruments they can have levelled the mountains and broken through the rocks to make them so broad and good as they are. . . . In some places, to secure the regular width, it was necessary to hew a path out of the living rock; all which was done with fire and their picks. In other places the ascents were so steep and high that steps had to be cut from below to enable the ascent to be made, with wider spaces at intervals for resting-places. In other parts there were great heaps of snow, which were more to be feared, and not at one spot only, but often recurring. Where these snows obstructed the way, and where there were forests of trees and loose clods of earth, the road was levelled and paved with stones when necessary. . . .

In the inhabited parts, near the towns, there were great palaces and lodgings for the soldiers. In the snowy wildernesses and plains, shelter-houses were built, where travellers could take refuge from the cold and rains. In many places, as in the Collao and other parts, there were distance-marks like the heaps in Europe which indicate boundaries, except that those in Peru are larger and better made. They called them *topos,* and the distance between them is a Castillian league and a half.

The manner of making these roads and their grandeur being understood, I will explain the ease with which they were constructed by the natives, without increasing the death-rate, or causing excessive labour. When any king determined to have any of these famous roads made, much preparation was not necessary, but it was merely needful that the king should give the order. For then the overseers went over the ground to make a trace, and the Indians received instructions to construct the road from among the inhabitants who were on either side. One province completed the section within its limits, and when it reached the boundary it was presently taken up by the next: and if it was urgent, they all worked at one time. When they reached the uninhabited parts, the Indians of the nearest inhabited districts brought provisions and tools, in such wise that, with much rejoicing and little fatigue, it was finished. For there was no apprehension, and the Yncas or their servants interfered in nothing.

They also made great paved causeways of excellent construction, such as that which passes by the valley of Xaquixaguana, leading from the city of Cuzco to Muhina. There were many of these royal roads, both in the mountains and along the coast. . . .

In the First Part I related how, in this kingdom of Peru, there was a very great quantity of flocks, both wild and tame, of . . . *pacos* [alpacas], *vicuñas*, and *llamas*, and excellent pastures in all parts, so that they could be well maintained. Although they were so numerous, it was forbidden by the kings, on pain of severe punishment, to kill females, and if the rule was broken, punishment followed, so that they were never eaten. They multiplied so that the number when the Spaniards arrived in the country is incredible. The principal reason for this order was to ensure the growth of sufficient wool to make clothing; for in many parts, if the flocks were wanting, I certainly do not know how the people could preserve themselves against the cold, if they had not any wool wherewith to make clothes. But by this arrangement there were many store-houses in all parts, where they kept the clothing, as well for the soldiers as for the rest of the people, and most of this cloth was made of the wool of guanacos and vicuñas.

When the lord desired to enjoy a royal hunt, it is noteworthy how many animals were taken and killed; as many as thirty thousand head. Tents were pitched in a position selected by the lord, on such occasions as he was pleased to amuse himself with the chase. For, on the high parts of the mountains, in whatever place was chosen, there were sure to be flocks in such quantities as we have stated.

Having assembled fifty thousand or sixty thousand people, they surrounded the plains and broken ground in such sort that they gradually approached each other, at the same time descending from the steeper heights to the more level plains, and making the country resound with the noise of their voices. Gradually they approached each other, until they formed a ring with hands joined, and in the enclosed space bounded by their bodies the flocks were detained and secured. The lord was so placed as to witness the slaughter. Then certain Indians entered the enclosure armed with *ayllos* [stones tied together with cords], which are used [by throwing] to secure the legs, and others with sticks and clubs, and began to seize and kill. Among the great quantity of captured animals there were many guanacos, which are rather larger than small donkeys, with long necks like camels. They tried to escape by spitting into the faces of the men and rushing about with great leaps. They say that it was a marvellous thing to hear the noise made by the Indians in catching them, and to see the efforts made by the animals to escape in all directions. If the king wished to kill any of the chase without entering into the tumult, it was arranged in any way he pleased.

Many days were passed in these hunts, and a multitude of animals were killed. Then the overseers ordered the wool to be taken to the store-houses, and to the temples of the Sun, where the *mamaconas* [women of the temples] were expert in making very fine cloth for the lords, the fineness being such that it appeared to be of silk, and of various colors. The flesh of the slaughtered animals was eaten by those who were present with the king, and some of it was dried in the sun, to be kept in the store-houses, as provisions for soldiers on the march. All these animals, it must be understood, were in wild flocks, and not domesticated. They also took many deer and *bisca-chas* [a large rodent], as well as foxes, and some bears and small lions.

One of the things for which one feels envious of these lords is their knowledge of the way to conquer the wild lands and to bring them, by good management, into the condition in which they were found by the Spaniards when they discovered this new kingdom. . . .

They always arranged matters, in the commencement of their negotiations, so that things should be pleasantly and not harshly ordered. Afterwards, some Incas inflicted severe punishments in many parts; but formerly, it is asserted on all sides, that they induced people to submit by great benevolence and friendliness. They marched from Cuzco with their army and warlike materials, until they were near the region they intended to conquer. Then they collected very complete information touching the power of the enemy, and whence help was likely to reach them, and by what road. This being known, the most effective steps were taken to prevent the succour from arriving, either by large bribes given to the allies, or by forcible resistance. At the same time forts were ordered to be constructed on heights or ridges, consisting of circles with high walls, one inside the other and each with a door. Thus if the outer one was lost, the defenders could retire into the next, and the next, until refuge was taken in the highest. They sent chosen men to examine the land, to see the roads, and learn by what means they were defended, as well as the places whence the enemy received supplies. When the road that should be taken and the necessary measures were decided upon, the Inca sent special messengers to the enemy to say that he desired to have them as allies and relations, so that, with joyful hearts and willing minds they ought to come forth to receive him in their province, and give him obedience as in the other provinces; and that they might do this of their own accord he sent presents to the native chiefs.

By this wise policy he entered into the possession of many lands without war. In that case, he gave orders to his soldiers that they should do no harm or injury, nor commit any robbery or act of violence; and if there were not sufficient provisions in the province, he ordered that it should be sent from other parts. For he desired that his sway should not appear heavy to those who had newly come under it, so as to know and hate him at the same time. If any newly conquered province had no flocks, he ordered that so many thousand heads should be sent there, to be well looked after, so as to multiply and supply wool to clothe the people; and none were to be killed for eating until the lapse of a certain number of years. If, on the other hand, they had flocks, but needed some other thing, a similar course was pursued to supply the want. If the people lived in caves or thickets, they were led, by kind words, to build houses and towns on the more level parts of the mountains; and when they were ignorant as regards the tilling of their land, they were instructed, and the method of making channels to irrigate their fields was taught to them.

In all things the system was so well regulated that when one of the Incas entered into a new province by friendly agreement, in a very short time it looked like another place, the natives yielding obedience and consenting that the royal governors and *mitimaes* [colonists] should remain with them. In many others, which were conquered by force of arms, the order was that little harm should be done to the property and houses of the vanquished; for the lord said, "These will soon be our people, as much as the others." For this reason the war was made with as little injury as possible, although great battles were often fought, where the inhabitants desired to retain their ancient liberty and their religion and customs, and not to adopt new ways. But during such wars the Incas always had the mastery, and when the enemies were vanquished, they were not destroyed; on the contrary, orders were given to release the captives and restore the spoils, and allow them to retain their estates. For the Inca desired to show them that they should not be so mad as to revolt against his royal person and reject his friendship; rather they should wish to be his friends, as were those in the other provinces. In saying this to them, he gave them beautiful women, pieces of rich cloth, and some gold.

With these gifts and kind words, he secured the good-will of all, in such sort that those who had fled into the wildernesses returned, without fear, to their houses, and all cast aside their weapons; while those who saw the Inca most frequently, looked upon themselves as most fortunate.

All were ordered to worship the Sun as their god. Their own customs and religious usages were not prohibited, but they were enjoined to conform to the laws and customs that were in force at Cuzco, and all were required to use the general language of the empire.

Having established a governor, with garrisons of soldiers, the army then advanced, and if the new provinces were large, it was presently ordered that a temple of the Sun should be built, and women collected for its service, and that a palace should be erected for the lord. Tribute was collected, care being taken that too much was not exacted, and that no injustice was done in anything; but that the new subjects were made acquainted with the imperial policy, with the art of building, of clothing themselves, and of living together in towns. And if they needed anything, care was taken to supply it, and to teach them how to sow and to cultivate their lands. So thoroughly was this policy carried into effect, that we know of many places where there were no flocks originally, but where there has been abundance since they were subjugated by the Incas; and others where formerly there was no maize, but where now they have large crops. In many provinces they went about like savages, badly clothed, and barefooted, until they came under the sway of the Incas; and from that time they have worn shirts and mantles, both men and women, so that they always hold the change in their memories. . . .

As in the last chapter I wrote of the method adopted by the Incas in their conquests, it will be well in this one to relate how they levied tribute from so many nations. It is a thing very well understood that there was no village, either in the mountains or in the valleys of the coast, which did not pay such tribute as was imposed by those who were in charge. It is said that when, in one province, the people represented that they had nothing wherewith to pay the tribute, the king ordered that each inhabitant should be obliged, every four months, to give a rather large cane full of live lice, which was a sign of the care taken by the Inca to make every subject contribute something. Thus we know that they paid their tribute of lice until such time as, having been supplied with flocks, they had been industrious enough to multiply them, and to make cloth wherewith to pay more suitable tribute in the time to come.

The system which the Orejones of Cuzco and the other native lords of the land say that the Incas adopted in imposing tribute was as follows: He who reigned in Cuzco, sent some of his principal officers to visit the empire, one by each of the four royal roads of which I have already written. One was called Chincha Suyo, which included all the provinces as far as Quito, with all the valleys of Chincha, towards the north. The second was Conde Suyo, which includes the provinces on the sea coast, and many in the mountains. The third was called Colla Suyo, including all the provinces to the south as far as Chile. The last road led to Ande Suyo, which included the lands covered with forests at the foot of mountains of the Andes.

So it was that when the lord desired to know what tribute would be due from all the provinces between Cuzco and Chile, along a road of such great length, as I have often explained, he ordered faithful persons whom he could trust, to go from village to village, examining the condition of the people and their capacity for payment. They also took note of the productiveness of the land, the quantity of flocks, the yield of metals, and of other things which they required and valued. Having performed this service with great diligence they returned to the lord to submit their reports. He then ordered a general assembly of the principal persons of the kingdom to meet. The lords of the provinces which had to pay the tribute being present, he addressed them lovingly, saying that as they received him as their sole lord and monarch of so many and such vast districts, they should take it in good part, without feeling it burdensome, to give the tribute that was due to the royal person, who would take care that it was moderate, and so light that they could easily pay it. Having been answered in conformity with his wishes, the lords of provinces returned to their homes, accompanied by certain Orejones who fixed the tribute. In some parts it was higher than is paid to the Spaniards at present. But, seeing that the system of the Incas was so perfect, the people did not feel the burden, rather increasing and multiplying in numbers and well being. . . .

When the officers sent by the Incas made their inspection, they entered a province and ascertained, by means of the *quipus,* the number of men and women, of old and young. Then they took account of the mines of gold and silver, and, with so many thousand Indians at work, the quantity that should be extracted was fixed. An order was given that such quantity should be delivered to the overseers. As those who were employed to work at the extraction of silver could not attend to the cultivation of their fields, the Inca imposed the duty upon the neighbouring province to find labour for the sowing and reaping of the crops of the miners. If the mining province was large, its own inhabitants were able both to carry on the mining works and to cultivate the ground. In case one of the miners fell ill, it was arranged that he should return to his home, and that another should take his place. No one was employed in the mines who was not married, because the wives had to supply their food and liquor; besides which, arrangements were made to send sufficient provisions to the mines. In this manner, although men might be at the mines all their lives, they were not overworked. Besides, there was provision to rest for certain days in each month, for their festivals and for pleasure. But in fact the same Indians did not always remain at the mines; for there were periodical reliefs.

The Incas so arranged the mining industry, that they extracted great abundance of gold and silver throughout the empire, and there must have been years when more than fifty thousand *arrobas* [one arroba weighs 25 pounds] of silver and fifteen thousand of gold were produced. It was always used for the royal service. The metal was brought to the principal place of the province, and in the manner that the mines were worked in one district in the same way were they ordered in all the others throughout the empire. If there were provinces where no metal could be extracted as a tribute, the people paid taxes in smaller things, and in women and boys, who were taken from the villages without causing any discontent. For if a man had an only child it was not taken, but if he had three or four children, one was required in payment of his dues.

Other provinces made their contributions in the form of so many thousand loads of maize, at each harvest. Others provided, on the same scale, a certain number of loads of dried *chuñus* [potatoes], in the same way as the maize, and others again paid in *quinua* [a grain], or other products. In other provinces the tribute consisted of so many cloth mantles, and in others of shirts, according to the number of inhabitants. Another form of tribute was the supply of so many thousand loads of lances, another of slings and *ayllos* [stones tied with cords], and all other kinds of weapons that they used. Other provinces were required to send so many thousand labourers to Cuzco, to be employed on the public edifices of the city and of the kings, with supplies of their needful provisions. Other provinces contributed cables to move the great stones, while others paid tribute in coca [a narcotic plant]. The system was so arranged that all the provinces of Peru paid something to the Incas in tribute, from the smallest to the most important. Such perfect regularity was maintained that while the people did not fail to provide what was required, those who made the collections never took even a grain of maize too much. All the provision and warlike stores that were contributed, were served out to the soldiers, or supplied to the garrisons which were formed in different parts, for the defence of the empire.

When there was no war, a large proportion was eaten and used by the poor; for when the kings were at Cuzco they were served by the *anaconas,* which is the name for perpetual servants who sufficed to till the royal fields, and do service in the palaces. Besides which, there was always brought for the royal table, from the provinces, many lambs [post-Spanish] and birds, fish, maize, coca, edible roots, and all kinds of fruits.

Such order was maintained in the tribute paid by the Indians that the Incas became very powerful, and never entered upon any war which did not extend their dominions.

To understand how, and in what manner, the tributes were paid, and the other taxes were collected, it must be known that in each *huata,* which is the name for a year, certain Orejones were sent as judges, but only with powers to inspect the provinces, and give notice to the inhabitants that if any felt aggrieved he was to state his complaints, in order that the officer who had done him the injury might be punished. Having received the complaints, and also ascertained whether any tribute had not been paid, the judges returned to Cuzco; whence others set out with power to inflict punishment on those who were in fault. Besides this, it was the rule that, from time to time, the principal men of the provinces should be permitted to appear before the lord, and report upon the condition of the provinces, on their needs, and on the incidence of taxation. Their representations then received attention, the Lords Incas being certain that they did not lie, but spoke the truth; for any deceit was severely punished, and in that case the tribute was increased. The women contributed by the provinces were divided between the service of the kings, and that of the temples of the Sun.

The Orejones who gave me information at Cuzco concurred in saying that formerly, in the time of the Kings Incas, orders were given throughout all the towns and provinces of Peru, that the principal lords and their lieutenants should take note, each year, of the men and women who had died, and also of the births. For as well for the assessment of tribute, as for calculating the number of men that could be called upon to serve as soldiers, and for the defence of the villages, such information was needed. This was easily done, because each province, at the end of the year, was ordered to set down in the *quipus,* by means of the knots, all the men who had died in it during the year, as well as all who were born. In the beginning of the following year, the *quipus* were taken to Cuzco, where an account was made of the births and deaths throughout the empire. These returns were prepared with great care and accuracy, and without any fraud or deceit. When the returns had been made up, the lord and his officers knew what people were poor, the number of widows, whether they were able to pay tribute, how many men could be taken for soldiers, and many other facts which were considered, among these people, to be of great importance.

As this empire was of such vast extent, a fact which I have frequently pointed out in many parts of this work, and as in each province there were a great number of storehouses for provisions and other necessaries for a campaign, and for the equipment of soldiers, if there was a war these great resources were used where the camps were formed, without touching the supplies of allies, or drawing upon the stores of different villages. If there was no war, all the great store of provisions was divided amongst the poor and the widows. The poor consisted of those who were too old to work, or who were maimed, lame, or infirm; but those who were well and able to work received nothing. Then the storehouses were again filled from the obligatory tributes; and if, by chance, there came a year of great sterility, the storehouses were, in like manner, ordered to be opened, and the necessary provisions were given out to the suffering provinces. But as soon as a year of plenty came, the deficiencies so caused were made up. Although the tributes given to the Incas did not serve for other purposes than the above, yet they were well expended, and the kingdom was well supplied and cared for. . . .

It is well known that the lords of this kingdom had their lieutenants or representatives in the principal places, in the time of their sovereign power. . . .

In these places there were larger houses and more resources than in many of the other towns of this great empire, so that they were the central positions or capitals of the provinces; for the tribute was brought into these centres from certain distant places at so many leagues distance to one, and at so many to another. The rules were so clear that every village knew to which centre it had to send its tribute. In all these capitals the kings had temples of the Sun, and houses with great store of plate, with people whose only duty it was to work at making rich pieces of gold and great vases of silver. There were also many soldiers as a garrison, and also a principal agent or lieutenant who was over all that came in, while he was expected to keep the account of all expenditure. These governors were not allowed to interfere in the administration of any neighbouring province; but within his own jurisdiction, if there was any disturbance or uproar, he had the power of inflicting punishment, much more if there was any treasonable movement or rebellion of one denying allegiance to the king. For it is certain that full powers were entrusted to these governors. . . .

When the Incas visited the provinces of their empire in time of peace, they travelled in great majesty, seated in rich litters fitted with loose poles of excellent wood, long and enriched with gold and silver work. Over the litter there were two high arches of gold set with precious stones, and long mantles fell round all sides of the litter so as to cover it completely. If the inmate did not wish to be seen, the mantles remained down, but they were raised when he got in or came out. In order that he might see the road, and have fresh air, holes were made in the curtains. Over all parts of these mantles or curtains there was rich ornamentation. On some were embroidered the sun and the moon, on others great curving serpents, and what appeared to be sticks passing across them. These were borne as insignia or arms. The litters were raised on the shoulders of the greatest and most important lords of the kingdom, and he who was employed most frequently on this duty, was held to be most honoured and in highest favour. . . .

The Incas, with a view to the efficient government of the empire, invented a system of posts, which was the best that could be thought of or imagined. . . .

There were built, from half-league to half-league, a little more or less, small houses well roofed with wood and straw; and among the mountains they were constructed against the rocks. Thus the roads were lined with these small houses at regular intervals. The order was that in each house there should be two Indians with provisions, stationed there by the neighbouring villages. They were not permanently left there, but were relieved by others from time to time; and the system of government was so efficient that it was only necessary to give the order, to ensure that these men should always be at their stations so long as the Incas reigned.

Each province took charge of the posts within its boundaries, including those which were on the coast deserts or in the region of snowy heights. When it was necessary to give notice to the kings in Cuzco, or in any other part, of any event that had taken place, or which was connected with their service, the men at the posts set out from Quito or Tomebamba, or from Chile or Caranqui, or from whatever other part of the empire, whether along the coast or in the mountains, and they ran with great speed, without stopping, each one over his half league. For the Indians who were stationed at the post houses, were chosen from among the most active and swiftest of all their countrymen. When one approached the next post house, he began to call out to the men who were in it, and to say:—"Start at once, and go to the next post with news that so and so has happened, which such a Governor wishes to announce to the Inca." When the other runner heard what was shouted to him, he started with the utmost speed, while the runner who arrived went into the house to rest, and to eat and drink of what was always kept in store there; while the other did, in like manner, at the next post house. . . .

In most, if not in all parts of the provinces of Peru there were and still are these *mitimaes,* and we understand that there were three classes of them. . . .

The first kind of *mitimaes,* as instituted by the Incas, were those who were moved to other countries, after a new province had been conquered. A certain number of the conquered people were ordered to people another land of the same climate and conditions as their original country. If it was cold, they were sent to a cold region, if warm, to a warm one, where they were given lands and houses such as those they had left. This was done that order might be secured, and that the natives might quickly understand how they must serve

and behave themselves, and learn all that the older vassals understood concerning their duties, to be peaceful and quiet, not hasty
to take up arms. At the same time, an equal number of settlers was
taken from a part which had been peaceful and civilized for a long
time, and sent into the newly conquered province, and among the
recently subjugated people. There they were expected to instruct
their neighbours in the ways of peace and civilization; and in this
way, both by the emigration of some and the arrival of others, all
was made secure under the royal governors and lieutenants.

The Incas knew how much all people feel the removal from their
country and their home associations, and in order that they might
take such banishment with good will, they did honour to those who
were selected as emigrants, gave bracelets of gold and silver to many
of them, and clothes of cloth and feathers to the women. They were
also privileged in many other ways. Among the colonists there were
spies, who took note of the conversations and schemes of the natives,
and supplied the information to the governors, who sent it to Cuzco
without delay, to be submitted to the Inca. In this way all was made
secure, for the natives feared the *mitimaes,* while the *mitimaes*
suspected the natives, and all learnt to serve and to obey quietly. If
there were turmoils or disturbances they were severely punished.
Among the Incas there were some who were revengeful, and who
punished without moderation and with great cruelty.

The *mitimaes* were employed to take charge of the flocks of the
Inca and of the Sun, others to make cloth, others as workers in
silver, and others as quarrymen and labourers. Some also were
sculptors and gravers of images; in short, they were required to do
such service as was most useful, and in the performance of which
they were most skilful. Orders were also given that *mitimaes* should
go into the forests of the Andes to sow maize and to cultivate coca
and fruit-trees. In this way the people of the regions where it was
too cold to grow these things were supplied with them.

The second class of *mitimaes* were those who formed garrisons
under captains, some of whom were *Orejones,* on the frontiers, in
forests east of the Andes. . . . In order that the burden of war
might not fall upon one tribe, and that they might not be able
quickly to concert a rising or rebellion, it was arranged that the
*mitimaes* should be taken from provinces that were conveniently

situated, to serve as soldiers in these garrisons; whose duty it was to hold and defend the forts, called *pucaras,* if it should be necessary. . . . The recompense for their service consisted in orders that were given on certain occasions, to bestow upon them woollen clothing, feathers, or bracelets of gold and silver, after they had shewn themselves to be valiant. They were also presented with women from among the great number that were kept, in each province, for the service of the Ynca, and as most of these were beautiful they were highly valued. . . .

The other manner of stationing *mitimaes* [of the third class] was more strange. . . . In the course of the conquests made by the Yncas, either in the mountains, or plains, or valleys, where a district appeared to be suitable for cultivation, with a good climate and fertile soil, which was still desert and uninhabited, orders were at once given that as many colonists as would be sufficient to people it should be brought from a neighbouring province with a similar climate. The land was then divided amongst them, and they were provided with flocks and all the provisions they needed, until they had time to reap their own harvests. These colonists worked so well, and the king required their labours to be proceeded with so diligently, that in a short time the new district was peopled and cultivated, insomuch that it caused great content to behold it. In this way many valleys on the coast and ravines on the mountains were peopled, both such as had been personally examined by the Yncas, and such as they knew of from report. No tribute was required from the new settlers for some years; and they were provided with women, provisions, and *coca,* that they might, with more goodwill, be induced to establish themselves in their new homes.

In this way there were very few cultivable lands that remained desert in the time of the Incas, but all were peopled, as is well known to the first Christians who entered the country. Assuredly, it causes no small grief to reflect that these Incas, being gentiles and idolaters, should have established such good order in the government and maintenance of such vast provinces, while we, being Christians, have destroyed so many kingdoms. For wherever the Christians have passed, discovering and conquering, nothing appears but destruction.

## 10 / THE FIRST SPANISH CONTACT WITH THE AZTECS OF MEXICO

*The Aztecs were the dominant economic, political, and military power in Mexico at the time Cortés arrived in 1519. They controlled not only central Mexico from the Pacific Ocean to the Gulf of Mexico, but had conducted successful military campaigns as far to the southeast as Guatemala. Their motives for aggression were principally two: to exact tribute from the conquered peoples; to take captives for future sacrifice in their capital, Tenochtitlán (Mexico City). They were caught in a vicious spiral of human sacrifice to their gods to insure victory in war, and the necessity of constantly fighting to obtain the sacrificial victims from their enemies. In contrast to the Incas of Peru, they made no attempt to acculturate the peoples they conquered to the Aztec way of life in preparation for full citizenship, but deliberately kept some of their close neighbors in the status of enemies in order to have a convenient source of sacrificial victims nearby. The Tlaxcalans had been raided by the Aztecs for decades for this purpose, which explains why they were so eager to join the ranks of Cortés in his campaign against the Aztecs.*

*Although the Spaniards were better armed, with their steel hand weapons, crossbows, guns, and cannon, their principal advantage over the Aztecs was psychological. Having fought the Moors constantly for almost eight hundred years from A.D. 711-1492, they took*

Bernal Díaz del Castillo, *The True History of the Conquest of Mexico*, trans. Maurice Keatinge (London: printed for J. Wright by John Dean, 1800), pp. 132-55.

*a very realistic attitude toward the problems of war. Montezuma, the foreign minister and war leader of the Aztec nation, was in a state of mental confusion, because he believed in the beginning that the Spaniards were the "White Gods" that an Aztec myth predicted would arrive. Therefore, at first he treated the Spaniards as friends and benefactors and apparently was not completely aware of their intentions until he became their captive. With the principal Aztec leader imprisoned and eventually killed, those remaining failed to keep up enough military pressure on the Spanish to defeat them.*

*Bernal Díaz was only a noncommissioned soldier in the ranks, but the Spanish force of between 400 and 450 men was so small that he had considerable face to face contact with both Cortés and Montezuma. Although Diaz wrote his account in his declining years in Spain half a century after the conquest of Mexico, it is by far the most graphic, colorful, and detailed description we have of Tenochtitlán and the leading characters in its drama.*

**Mexico, Nov. 8th, 1519.**

*Description of that Court and City.*
*Transactions and Occurrences there.*

On the next day we set out, accompanied as on the former one, and proceeded by the grand causeway, which is eight yards wide, and runs in a straight line to the city of Mexico. It was crowded with people, as were all the towers, temples, and causeways, in every part of the lake, attracted by curiosity to behold men, and animals, such as never had been before seen in these countries. We were occupied by very different thoughts; our number did not amount to four hundred and fifty, we had perfectly in our recollection the accounts we had received on our march, that we were to be put to death on our arrival in the city which we now saw before us, approachable only by causeways, whereon were several bridges, the breaking of one of which effectually cut off our retreat. And now let who can, tell me, where are men in this world to be found except ourselves, who would have hazarded such an attempt?

When we arrived at a place where a small causeway turns off, which goes to the city of Cuyoacan, we were met by a great number of the lords of the court in their richest dresses, sent as they said before the great Montezuma, to bid us welcome. After waiting there some time, the nephew of Montezuma and other noblemen went back to meet their monarch, who approached, carried in a most magnificent litter, which was supported by his principal nobility. When we came near certain towers which are almost close to the city, Montezuma who was then there quitted his litter, and was borne in the arms of the princes of Tezcuco, Iztapalapa, Tacuba, and Cuyoacan, under a canopy of the richest materials, ornamented with green feathers, gold, and precious stones that hung in the manner of fringe; he was most richly dressed and adorned, and wore buskins of pure gold ornamented with jewels. The princes who supported him were dressed in rich habits, different from those in which they came to meet us, and others who preceded the monarch spread mantles on the ground, lest his feet should touch it. All who attended him, except the four princes, kept their eyes fixed upon the earth, not daring to look him in the face.

When Cortes was told that the great Montezuma approached, he dismounted from his horse, and advanced towards him with much respect; Montezuma bid him welcome, and Cortes replied with a compliment, and it appeared to me, that he offered to yield the right hand to Montezuma, who declined it, and put Cortes on his right. Our general then produced a collar of those artificial jewels called margajitas, which are of various colors, set in gold, and threw it upon the neck of Montezuma; after which, he advanced to embrace him, but the lords who surrounded the monarch, taking him by the arm, prevented him, it appearing to them not sufficiently respectful. Cortes then said, that he rejoiced in having seen so great a monarch, and that he was highly honored by his coming out to meet him, as well as by the many other marks of his favor. To this Montezuma made a gracious reply, and gave orders to the princes of Tezcuco and Cuyoacan to attend us to our quarters. Attended by his nobility, he then returned to the city, all the people standing close to the walls, without daring to lift up their eyes, and thus we passed, without obstruction from the crowd. Who could count the multitude of men, women, and children, which thronged the streets, the canals, and terraces on the tops of the houses, on that day! The whole of what I saw on this occasion is so strongly imprinted in my memory, that it appears to me as if it had happened only yesterday: glory to our Lord Jesus Christ, who gave us courage to venture upon such dangers, and brought us safely through them!

And praised be he, that he has suffered me to live, to write this my true history, although not so fully and satisfactorily as the subject deserves.

Our lodgings were provided in the buildings which had been inhabited by the father of Montezuma; here the monarch had the temples of his gods, and a secret treasure of gold and valuables, which he had derived from his father Axayaca. We were lodged here, because being considered as Teules [gods; literally, devils], they thought we were in our proper place amongst their idols. Be it how it may however, here they brought us to lodge in large apartments, a raised platform being assigned for our general, and mats for each of us, with little canopies over them, such as are used in that country. The whole of this palace was very light, airy, clean, and pleasant, the entry being through a great court. Montezuma here led Cortes by the hand to the apartment destined for him, and taking a large collar of gold, placed it round the general's neck. Cortes declared his gratitude for these favors, and Montezuma said, "Malintzin [the Indian woman who interpreted for the Spanish], here you and your friends are at home; now repose yourselves." With these words he departed. We were allotted to our quarters by companies, our artillery was posted in a convenient place, and all was arranged in such a manner as to be prepared for any contingency; a very sumptuous entertainment was provided for us, which we sat down to with great satisfaction, and here ends the true and full account of our adventurous and magnanimous entry into Mexico, on the eighth day of November, in the year of our Lord 1519. Glory be to Jesus Christ for all!

When the great Montezuma had made his repast, and understood that we had done the same, attended by a great body of his nobility he came to our apartments. Cortes went out to the middle of the hall to receive him, where Montezuma took him by the hand, and seats richly ornamented being brought, they both sat down, by the desire of the king, who then began a very pertinent speech, wherein he observed, that he rejoiced to have in his dominions captains so brave as Cortes and his associates; that he had before heard of one who had arrived at Champoton, and also of another who had come with four ships in the preceding year; that he had been anxious to see them, but had been disappointed: now however that we were arrived, he was happy to offer us all the favor he had in his power to bestow, for we were undoubtedly those who had been mentioned by his ancestors, who had predicted, that there would come certain men, from that part where the sun rises, to govern these countries; and it could mean no other but us, who had fought so valiantly since our arrival in their country; a representation of each of our battles having been sent to him. Cortes replied, that he and all of us never could repay the great favors we every day received from his hands: that we certainly were those of whom it had been prophecied, and that we were vassals of a potent monarch named Don Carlos, who had many and great princes subject to him, and had sent us, hearing of the fame and grandeur of king Montezuma, to request in his name, that the great Montezuma and his subjects would embrace the holy christian faith, which is the faith professed by our monarch, by doing which he would preserve the souls of him, his family, and subjects; and that he should in good time be informed of more particulars, such as that we worshipped the only true God, with many other things highly edifying to the hearers. This conversation being concluded, Montezuma presented our general with a quantity of valuable ornaments of wrought gold; to each of the captains he made a present of some gold and three loads of mantles, and to each soldier of two loads of richly wrought mantles; and all this he did in the most free and gracious manner, or to speak most properly, like a great monarch as he was. Montezuma then asked Cortes if his soldiers were all brothers, and vassals of our emperor. To which Cortes replied, that we were all brothers in love and friendship, persons of consequence in our own country, and servants of our sovereign lord the king. With mutual compliments Montezuma then departed, having given orders to his officers to provide us amply according to our demands, with corn, stone mills, and women to make bread, together with fowls, and fruit, and plenty of grass for the horses.

The next day was fixed on by Cortes, for his visit to Montezuma. Accordingly, attended by Captains Pedro de Alvarado, Juan Velasquez de Leon, Diego de Ordas, Gonzalo de Sandoval, and five soldiers, he went to his palace, which as soon as Montezuma was informed of, he came as far as the middle of the hall to meet us, attended by his relations, no other persons being allowed to enter where he was, except on most important business. With great ceremony on each side, the king took Cortes by the hand, and leading him to the elevated part of the saloon, placed him upon his right, and with much affability, desired the rest of us to be seated. Cortes then proceeded to say, that he came to him for the service of the Lord God whom the christians adored, who was named Jesus Christ, and who suffered death for our sakes. He also explained to him, that we adored the cross as the emblem of the crucifixion for our salvation, whereby the human race was redeemed, and that our Lord on the third day rose, and is in heaven, and that it is he who created heaven, and earth, and sea, and is adored by us as our Creator; but that those things which he [Montezuma] held to be gods, were not such, but devils, which are very bad things, of evil countenances, and worse deeds; and that he might judge how wicked they were, and how little power they had, in as much as where ever we placed crosses, they dare not shew their faces. He therefore requested, that he would attend to what he had told him, which was, that we were all brothers, the children of Adam and Eve, and that as such, our emperor lamenting the loss of souls in such numbers as those which were brought by his idols into everlasting flames, had sent us to apply a remedy thereto, by putting an end to the worship of these false gods, to human sacrifices, and all other crimes; and that he now came to notify his Majesty's intentions, but our emperor would at a future period send holy men, fully capable of explaining them.

Here Cortes stopped, and Montezuma seemed to shew an inclination to reply, but Cortes observing that this was enough for the first time, proposed to us to retire, and we were preparing to do so, when we were prevented by Montezuma who spoke to him as follows. "Malintzin, I have already heard through my ambassadors of those things which you now mention, and to which hitherto we have made no reply, because we have from the first worshipped the gods we now do, and consider them as just and good. So no doubt are yours. In regard to the creation of the world, our beliefs are the same, and we also believe you to be the people who were to come to us from where the sun rises. To your great king I am indebted. There have been already persons on our coasts, from your country; I wish to know if you are all the same people." To which Cortes having replied that they were all subjects of the same prince, Montezuma said, that from the first time he heard of them, it had been his wish to see them, which his gods had now granted him; that we should therefore consider ourselves as at home, and if ever we were refused entrance into any of his cities, it was not his fault, but that of his subjects, who were terrified by the reports they heard of us, such as that we carried with us thunder and lightning, that our horses killed men, and that we were furious Teules, with other follies of that kind; adding, that he saw we were men, that we were valiant and wise, for which he esteemed us, and would give us proofs thereof. He then addressed himself to Cortes in a laughing manner, for he was very gay in conversation when he was in his state, saying, "Malintzin, the Tlascalans your new friends have I know told you that I am like a god, and that all about me is gold, and silver, and precious stones; but you now see that I am mere flesh and blood, and that my houses are built like other houses, of lime and stone, and timber. It is true that I am a great king, and inherit riches from my ancestors; but for these ridiculous falsehoods, you treat them with the same contempt, that I do the stories I was told of your commanding the elements." To which Cortes good-humouredly replied, that the accounts of enemies were not to be relied on, paying him at the same time a handsome compliment, upon his power and grandeur. During this conversation Montezuma had made a sign to one of his principal attendants, to order his officers to bring him certain pieces of gold, which he had laid apart to give to Cortes, together with ten loads of fine stuffs, which he divided between Cortes and his captains, and to every soldier he gave two collars of gold, each worth ten crowns, and two loads of mantles. The gold amounted in value to upwards of a thousand crowns; and he gave it with an affability, and indifference, which made him appear a truly magnificent prince. It being now past midday, Cortes took his leave, observing that it was his Majesty's hour of dinner, and that he heaped obligations upon us; to which Montezuma replied, that on the contrary we had obliged him. We then retired, impressed with respect for the great Montezuma, from his princely manners and liberality.

The great Montezuma was at this time aged about forty years, of good stature, well proportioned, and thin: his complexion was much fairer than that of the Indians; he wore his hair short, just covering his ears, with very little beard, well arranged, thin, and black. His face was rather long, with a pleasant countenance, and good eyes; gravity and good humour were blended together when he spoke. He was very delicate and clean in his person, bathing himself every evening. He had a number of mistresses, of the first families, and two princesses his lawful wives: when he visited them, it was with such secrecy, that none could know it except his own servants. He was clear of all suspicion of unnatural vices. The clothes which he wore one day, he did not put on for four days after. He had two hundred of his nobility as a guard, in apartments adjoining his own. Of these, certain persons only, could speak to him, and when they went to wait upon him they took off their rich mantles, and put on others of less ornament, but clean. They entered his apartment barefooted, their eyes fixed on the ground, and making three inclinations of the body as they approached him. In addressing the king they said, "Lord, my lord, great lord." When they had finished he dismissed them with a few words, and they retired, with their faces towards him, and their eyes fixed upon the ground. I also observed, that when great men came from a distance about business, they entered his palace barefooted, and in a plain habit; and also, that they did not enter the gate directly, but took a circuit in going towards it.

His cooks had upwards of thirty different ways of dressing meats, and they had earthen vessels so contrived as to keep them always hot. For the table of Montezuma himself, above three hundred dishes were dressed, and for his guards, above a thousand. Before dinner, Montezuma would sometimes go out and inspect the preparations, and his officers would point out to him which were the best, and explained of what birds and flesh they were composed; and of those he would eat. But this was more for amusement than any thing else. It is said that at times the flesh of young children was dressed for him; but the ordinary meats were, domestic fowls, pheasants, geese, partridges, quails, venison, Indian hogs, pigeons, hares, and rabbits, with many other animals and birds peculiar to the country. This is certain; that after Cortes had spoken to him relative to the dressing human flesh, it was not practised in his palace. At his meals, in the cold weather, a number of torches of the bark of a wood which makes no smoke and has an aromatic smell, were lighted, and that they should not throw too much heat, screens, ornamented with gold, and painted with figures of idols, were placed before them. Montezuma was seated on a low throne, or chair, at a table proportioned to the height of his seat. The table was covered with white cloths and napkins, and four beautiful women presented him with water for his hands, in vessels which they call Xicales, with other vessels under them like plates, to catch the water; they also presented him with towels. Then, two other women brought small cakes of bread, and when the king began to eat, a large screen of wood, gilt, was placed before him, so that people should not during that time see him. The women having retired to a little distance, four ancient lords stood by the throne, to whom Montezuma from time to time spoke or addressed questions, and as a mark of particular favor, gave to each of them a plate of that which he was eating. I was told that these old lords, who were his near relations, were also counsellors and judges. The plates which Montezuma presented to them, they received with high respect, eating what was in them without taking their eyes off the ground. He was served on earthenware of Cholula, red and black. While the king was at table, no one of his guards, or in the vicinity of his apartment, dared for their lives make any noise. Fruit of all the kinds that the country produced was laid before him; he eat very little, but from time to time, a liquor prepared from cocoa, and of a stimulative, or corroborative quality, as we were told, was presented to him in golden cups. We could not at that time see if he drank it or not, but I observed a number of jars, above fifty, brought in, filled with foaming chocolate, of which he took some, which the women presented to him. At different intervals during the time of dinner, there entered certain Indians, hump-backed, very deformed, and ugly, who played tricks of buffoonery, and others who they said were jesters. There was also a company of singers and dancers, who afforded Montezuma much entertainment. To these he ordered the vases of chocolate to be distributed. The four female attendants then took away the cloths, and again with much respect presented him with water to wash his hands, during which time Montezuma conversed with the four old noblemen formerly mentioned, after which they took their leave with many ceremonies. One thing I forgot, and no wonder, to mention in its place, and that is, that during the time Montezuma was at dinner, two very beautiful women were busily employed making small cakes with eggs and other things mixed therein. These were delicately white, and when made they presented them to him on plates covered with napkins. Also another kind of bread was brought to him in long loaves, and plates of cakes resembling wafers. After he had dined, they presented to him three little canes highly ornamented, containing liquid amber, mixed with an herb they call tobacco; and when he had sufficiently viewed and heard the singers, dancers, and buffoons, he took a little of the smoke of one of these canes, and then laid himself down to sleep; and thus his principal meal concluded. After this was over, all his guards and domestics sat down to dinner, and as near as I could judge, above a thousand plates of those eatables that I have mentioned were laid before them, with vessels of foaming chocolate, and fruit in an immense quantity. For his women and various inferior servants, his establishment was of a prodigious expence; and we were astonished, amidst such a profusion, at the vast regularity that prevailed. His major domo was at this time a prince named Tapiea; he kept the accounts of Montezuma's rents, in books which occupied an entire house. Montezuma had two buildings filled with every kind of arms, richly ornamented with gold and jewels, such as shields large and small, clubs like two-handed swords, and lances much larger than ours, with blades six feet in length, so strong that if they fix in a shield they do not break, and sharp enough to use as razors. There was also an immense quantity of bows and arrows, and darts, together with slings, and shields which roll up into a small compass, and in action are let fall and thereby cover the whole body. He had also much defensive armour of quilted cotton ornamented with feathers in different devices, and casques for the head, made of wood and bone, with plumes of feathers, and many other articles too tedious to mention.

In this palace was a most magnificent aviary, which contained every description of birds that continent afforded, namely, royal eagles, and a smaller species, with many other birds, down to the smallest parroquets, of beautiful colors. It was here that the ornaments of green feathers were fabricated. The feathers were taken from birds which are of the size of our pyes in Spain, and which they call here Quetzales, and other birds, whose plumage is of five different colours, green, red, white, yellow, and blue. Here was also an immensity of parrots, and certain geese of fine plumage, and a species which resembled geese. All these bred here, and were stripped of their feathers every year at the proper season. Here was a large pond of clear running water, where were a number of great birds, entirely red, with very long legs; there are some like them in the Island of Cuba, which they call Ipiris. There was also a species which lives entirely in the water.

We likewise saw another great building, which was a temple, and which contained those which were called the valiant or fighting gods, and here were many kinds of furious beasts, tygers, and lions of two species, one of which resembles a wolf, called here Adive. Also foxes, and other smaller animals, but all carnivorous. Most of these were bred in the place, being fed with game, fowls, dogs, and as I have heard the bodies of Indians who were sacrificed, the manner of which as I have been informed is this. They open the body of the victim while living, with large knives of stone; they take out his heart, and blood, which they offer to their gods, and then they cut off the limbs, and the head, upon which they feast, giving the body to be devoured by the wild beasts, and the skulls they hang up in their temples. In this accursed place were many vipers, and poisonous serpents [rattlesnakes] which have in their tails somewhat that sounds like castanets; these are the most dangerous of all, and were kept in vessels filled with feathers, where they reared their young, and were fed with the flesh of human beings, and dogs; and I have been assured, that after our expulsion from Mexico, all these animals lived for many days upon the bodies of our comrades who were killed on that occasion. These beasts and horrid reptiles were retained to keep company with their infernal gods, and when these animals yelled and hissed, the palace seemed like hell itself.

The place where the artists principally resided was named Escapuzalco, and was at the distance of about a league from the city. Here were the shops and manufactories of all their gold and silver smiths, whose works in these metals, and in jewellery, when they were brought to Spain, surprised our ablest artists. Their painters we may also judge of by what we now see, for there are three Indians in Mexico, who are named, Marcos de Aquino, Juan de la Cruz, and Crespillo, who, if they had lived with Apelles in ancient times, or were compared with Michael Angelo or Berruguete in modern times, would not be held inferior to them. Their fine manufactures of cotton and feathers, were principally brought from the province of Costitlan. The women of the family of the great Montezuma also, of all ranks, were extremely ingenious in these works, and constantly employed; as was a certain description of females who lived together in the manner of nuns.

One part of the city was entirely occupied by Montezuma's dancers, of different kinds, some of whom bore a stick on their feet, others flew in the air, and some danced like those in Italy called by us Matachines. He had also a number of carpenters and handicraft men constantly in his employ. His gardens, which were of great extent, were irrigated by canals of running water, and shaded with every variety of trees. In them were baths of cut stone, pavilions for feasting or retirement, and theatres for shows, and for the dancers and singers; all which were kept in the most exact order, by a number of labourers constantly employed.

When we had been four days in Mexico, Cortes wished to take a view of the city, and in consequence sent to request the permission of his Majesty. Accordingly, Aguilar, Donna Marina [Malintzin], and a little page of our general's called Orteguilla, who already understood something of the language, went to the palace for that purpose. Montezuma was pleased immediately to accede, but being apprehensive that we might offer some insult to his temple, he determined to go thither in person, which he accordingly did, in the same form, and with the same retinue, as when he first came out to meet us, but that he was on this occasion preceded by two lords bearing sceptres in their hands, which they carried on high, as a signal of the king's approach. Montezuma, in his litter, with a small rod in his hand, one half of which was gold, and the other half wood, and which he bore elevated like a rod of justice, for such it was, approached the temple, and there quitted his litter and mounted the steps, attended by a number of priests, and offering incense, with many ceremonies, to his war gods. Cortes at the head of his cavalry, and the principal part of our soldiers under arms, marched to the grand square, attended by many noblemen of the court. When we arrived there, we were astonished at the crowds of people, and the regularity which prevailed, as well as at the vast quantities of merchandise, which those who attended us were assiduous in pointing out. Each kind had its particular place, which was distinguished by a sign. The articles consisted of gold, silver, jewels, feathers, mantles, chocolate, skins dressed and undressed, sandals, and other manufactures of the roots and fibres of nequen, and great numbers of male and female slaves, some of whom were fastened by the neck, in collars, to long poles. The meat market was stocked with fowls, game, and dogs. Vegetables, fruits, articles of food ready dressed, salt, bread, honey, and sweet pastry made in various ways, were also sold here. Other places in the square were appointed to the sale of earthenware, wooden household furniture such as tables and benches, firewood, paper, sweet canes filled with tobacco mixed with liquid amber, copper axes and working tools, and wooden vessels highly painted. Numbers of women sold fish, and little loaves made of a certain mud which they find in the lake, and which resembles cheese. The makers of stone blades were busily employed shaping them out of the rough material, and the merchants who dealt in gold, had the metal in grains as it came from the mines, in transparent tubes [quills], so that they could be reckoned, and the gold was valued at so many mantles, or so many xiquipils of cocoa, according to the size of the quills. The entire square was inclosed in piazzas, under which great quantities of grain were stored, and where were also shops for various kinds of goods. I must apologize for adding, that boat loads of human ordure were on the borders of the adjoining canals, for the purpose of tanning leather, which they said could not be done without it. Some may laugh at this, but I assert the fact is as I have stated it, and moreover, upon all the public roads, places for passengers to resort to, were built of canes, and thatched with straw or grass, in order to collect this material.

The courts of justice, where three judges sat, occupied a part of the square, their under officers being in the market, inspecting the merchandise.

From the square we proceeded to the great temple, but before we entered it we made a circuit through a number of large courts, the smallest of which appeared to me to contain more ground than the great square in Salamanca, with double inclosures built of lime and stone, and the courts paved with large white cut stone, very clean; or where not paved, they were plaistered and polished. When we approached the gate of the great temple, to the flat summit of which the ascent was by a hundred and fourteen steps, and before we had mounted one of them, Montezuma sent down to us six priests, and two of his noblemen, to carry Cortes up, as they had done their sovereign, which he politely declined. When we had ascended to the summit of the temple, we observed on the platform as we passed, the large stones whereon were placed the victims who were to be sacrificed. Here was a great figure which resembled a dragon, and much blood fresh spilt. Montezuma came out from an adoratory in which his accursed idols were placed, attended by two priests, and addressing himself to Cortes, expressed his apprehension that he was fatigued; to which Cortes replied, that fatigue was unknown to us.

Montezuma then took him by the hand, and pointed out to him the different parts of the city, and its vicinity, all of which were commanded from that place. Here we had a clear prospect of the three causeways by which Mexico communicated with the land, and of the aqueduct of Chapultepeque, which supplied the city with the finest water. We were struck with the numbers of canoes, passing to and from the main land, loaded with provisions and merchandise, and we could now perceive, that in this great city, and all the others of that neighbourhood which were built in the water, the houses stood separate from each other, communicating only by small drawbridges, and by boats, and that they were built with terraced tops. We observed also the temples and adoratories of the adjacent cities, built in the form of towers and fortresses, and others on the causeway, all whitewashed, and wonderfully brilliant. The noise and bustle of the market-place below us could be heard almost a league off, and those who had been at Rome and at Constantinople said, that for convenience, regularity, and population, they had never seen the like. Cortes now proposed to Fra. Bartholome to apply to Montezuma for permission to construct our church here, to which the father for the present objected, thinking it ill-timed. Cortes then addressing himself to Montezuma, requested that he would do him the favour to shew us his gods. Montezuma having first consulted his priests, led us into a tower where was a kind of saloon. Here were two altars highly adorned, with richly wrought timbers on the roof, and over the altars, gigantic figures resembling very fat men. The one on the right was Huitzilopochtli their war god, with a great face and terrible eyes; this figure was entirely covered with gold and jewels, and his body bound with golden serpents; in his right hand he held a bow, and in his left a bundle of arrows. The little idol which stood by him represented his page, and bore a lance and target richly ornamented with gold and jewels. The great idol had round his neck the figures of human heads and hearts, made of pure gold and silver, ornamented with precious stones of a blue colour. Before the idol was a pan of incense, with three hearts of human victims which were then burning, mixed with copal. The whole of that apartment, both walls and floor, was stained with human blood in such quantity as to give a very offensive smell. On the left was the other great figure, with a countenance like a bear, and great shining eyes, of the polished substance [obsidian] whereof their mirrors are made. The body of this idol was also covered with jewels. These two deities, it was said, were brothers; the name of this last was Tezcatepuca, and he was the god of the infernal regions. He presided, according to their notions, over the souls of men. His body was covered with figures representing little devils with tails of serpents, and the walls and pavement of this temple were so besmeared with blood that they stunk worse than all the slaughter-houses of Castille. An offering lay before him of five human hearts. In the summit of the temple, and in a recess the timber of which was most highly ornamented, we saw a figure half human and the other half resembling an alligator, inlaid with jewels, and partly covered with a mantle. This idol was said to contain the germ, and origin of all created things, and was the god of harvest, and fruits. The walls and altars were bestained like the rest, and so offensive, that we thought we never could get out soon enough.

In this place they had a drum of most enormous size, the head of which was made of the skins of large serpents: this instrument when struck resounded with a noise that could be heard to the distance of two leagues, and so doleful that it deserved to be named the music of the infernal regions; and with their horrible sounding horns and trumpets, their great knives for sacrifice, their human victims, and their blood besprinkled altars, I devoted them, and all their wickedness to God's vengeance, and thought that the time would never arrive, that I should escape from this scene of human butchery, horrible smells, and more detestable sights.

Cortes, half in jest, addressing himself to Montezuma, expressed his wonder how so wise a prince could worship such absurd and wicked powers; and proposed to him to place on the summit of that tower a cross, and in these adoratories the image of the holy Virgin, and he assured him that he should then be soon convinced of the vanity and deception of his idols. Montezuma shewed marks of displeasure at these expressions, saying, that he would not have admitted us into the temple, had he thought that we would have insulted their gods, who were kind to them, who gave them health and seasonable rains, good harvests, fine weather, victories and whatever else they desired, and whom they were in duty, and in gratitude, bound to worship. Cortes dropped the discourse, observing that it was time for us to go; and Montezuma assenting, said, it was necessary for him to remain, to expiate by sacrifice the sin which he had committed, in admitting us there. Cortes then took leave, and thus we concluded our visit to the great temple of Mexico, descending the steps with much pain to our invalids.

I will now proceed to relate other matters, in which, if I am not so correct as I ought to be, let it be remembered that my situation was that of a soldier, who was obliged to be more attentive to the orders of his officer, than to the objects of curiosity around him. The ground whereon this temple stood, was as much as six of the largest buildings of this country occupy. From the base it diminished to the summit, whereon was a tower, in which the idols were placed, and from the middle of the ascent, to the top, were five concavities, like barbicans, but without parapets. However there are many paintings of temples in the possession of the conquerors, one whereof I have, and those who have seen them will easily form an idea of the outside of this temple. I have heard that at the time they laid the foundations of it, the natives of all that country made offerings of their gold, silver, and jewels, of the seeds of the earth, and of prisoners, all which were buried in the foundations of the building. The inquisitive reader will naturally ask, how I came to know any thing of this, which happened upwards of a thousand years ago. I will inform him. When we got possession of this great city, and that it was to be built upon a new plan, it was determined to place the church of St. Jago on the ground where this temple stood; and in sinking the foundations, we found great quantities of gold, silver, and other valuables, and a Mexican who obtained part of the same ground, discovered more treasure, about which there was a law-suit in support of his Majesty's right, the result of which I am ignorant of. The account was also confirmed by Guatimotzin who was then alive, and who said that the transaction was recorded in their ancient historical paintings. The church which now stands here is called St. Jago el Taltelulco. This temple I have before observed, was surrounded by courts as large as the square of Salamanca, inside of a double inclosure of lime and stone. At a little distance from it stood a tower, a true hell or habitation for demons, with a mouth resembling that of an enormous monster, wide open, and ready as it were to devour those who entered. At the door stood frightful idols; by it was a place for sacrifice, and within, boilers, and pots full of water, to dress the flesh of the victims, which was eaten by the priests. The idols were like serpents and devils, and before them were tables and knives for sacrifice, the place being covered with the blood which was spilt on those occasions. The furniture was like that of a butcher's stall, and I never gave this accursed building any name except that of hell. Having passed this, we saw great piles of wood, and a reservoir of water, supplied by a pipe from the great aqueduct; and crossing a court, we came to another temple, wherein were the tombs of the Mexican nobility; it was begrimed with soot and blood. Next to this was another, full of skeletons, and piles of bones, each kept apart, but regularly arranged. In each temple were idols, and each had also its particular priests, who wore long vestments of black, somewhat between the dress of the dominicans and our canons; their long hair was clotted together, and their ears lacerated in honor of their gods.

At a certain distance from the buildings of which I have last spoken were others, the idols of which were, as they said, the advocates, or superintendent deities of human marriages, and all round the great court were many houses, which were not very lofty, and wherein resided the priests, and others who had charge of the idols. Here was also a great reservoir of water, supplied with pipes, exclusively for the service of the two idols Huitzilopochtli and Tezcatepuca, and hard by, a large building, where were a number of the young Mexican women, who resided there as in a nunnery, until they were married. They worshipped two female deities, who presided over marriages, and to them they offered sacrifices, in order to obtain good husbands. I have been thus diffuse in my description of this great temple, because it was the most considerable in that city, amongst the many sumptuous buildings of that kind which it contained. The temple of Cholula however was higher than this, having a hundred and twenty steps; it was also held in great veneration, and was built on a plan different from that of Mexico. The temple at Tezcuco was very large, having a hundred and seventeen steps. All these were of different structure, but agreed in having a number of outer courts, and a double inclosure. One ridiculous circumstance is, that each province had its own peculiar gods, who were supposed to have no concern with any other; so that the idols were innumerable in this country. Having fatigued ourselves with the examination of these scenes, so new to us, we retired to our quarters.

Cortes perceiving how adverse the king was to the conversion of his temple into a christian church, applied to one of the principal officers of his palace, for materials to construct a chapel and altar, within our quarters. His desire being made known to Montezuma, it was instantly complied with, and timber and workmen being provided, in three days we had it completed. Here we said mass every day; we had however to lament the total want of wine for the holy sacrament, it having been all used in the illness of Cortes, the reverend father, and others, during the wars in Tlascala. However we were constant in our devotions, as well on account of our duty, as in order to impress a proper idea of our holy religion, on the minds of Montezuma and the natives. Being employed in looking out for a proper place to fix the holy cross, one of our carpenters observed an appearance on the wall, as if a door had been there, and lately closed up. When this was made known to Cortes, it was privately opened, and on entering the apartment, they found riches without end! The secret soon transpired, and we went, all of us, to view them. I was then a young man, and I thought that if all the treasures of the earth had been brought into one place, they could not have amounted to so much. It was agreed to close up the door again, and we determined to conceal the knowledge of it until the proper time should offer.

A council was now called, composed of Cortes as president, with four captains, and twelve soldiers whereof I was one, and having duly considered how evidently the Lord guided us, and what wise and valiant captains and brave soldiers we had, as also the fickle disposition of the Indians, who though now kind to us, might change, there was no saying how soon, and that notwithstanding the hospitality with which Montezuma treated us, he might at any moment fall into an opposite line of conduct, we resolved to follow the opinion of Cortes, by adopting the most effectual measure, which was, to seize, and make that monarch our prisoner; as we could not know at what moment we might be perhaps poisoned in our food, and as no gift of his, nor all his father's treasure, could make compensation to us for the alarms, and distressing thoughts, which filled the minds of those of any reflection. For these reasons it was therefore agreed to adopt the measure without delay. The captains who were present proposed, that Montezuma should be induced by a plausible pretext to come into our quarters, and when there, to seize him, and if he resisted, to make his person answer it: and they urged, that of the two great dangers, this was much the least. It was then observed by some of our soldiers, that Montezuma's officers did not provide us so plentifully as at the first, and two of our Tlascalan allies had told our interpreter, Aguilar, in confidence, that they observed a bad disposition on the part of the Mexicans towards us, for the two last days. This debate lasted a full hour; at length it was agreed to adjourn until the next day, and in the mean time we consulted our reverend father of the order of mercy, praying to God to guide us in this difficulty. On the day after this debate, arrived two Indians of Tlascala very secretly, with letters from Villa Rica, whereby we were informed, that Juan de Escalante had fallen, together with six soldiers, in a battle with the Mexicans, and that the inhabitants of the mountains and of Cempoal were in commotion, and refused to supply provisions, or to work, so that the garrison knew not what to do. These letters added, that the opinion of the Indians were much altered since they found that the Spaniards could be killed like other men. God knows this intelligence afflicted us; it was the first defeat that we had experienced since we landed on that continent; and here let the reflecting reader ponder upon the changes which fate makes in the affairs of men. We who yesterday were honored by Montezuma, in possession of wealth, and considered invulnerable like demigods, to day found ourselves lowered in the consideration of the natives to a level with them in whose power we were. We now therefore saw in a stronger point of view than ever, how necessary it was for our very existence to seize Montezuma, and that if we failed, we might as well perish in the attempt as meet our certain fate in any other ways. . . .

It having been decided that we should seize the person of the king, we passed the whole of the preceding night in praying to our Lord, that he would be pleased to guide us so that what we were about to do should redound to his holy service, and in the morning we proceeded to arrange the manner in which our determination was to be carried into effect. Our cavalry and infantry were as usual in readiness to turn out if called upon, and as it was always our custom to go fully armed, the appearance in that manner gave no suspicion. Cortes having left our whole force in readiness, proceeded to the palace, attended by the captains, P. de Alvarado, Gonzalo de Sandoval, J. V. de Leon, Fra. de Lugo, and A. de Avila, with the interpreters Donna Marina and Aguilar; sending before him to acquaint the king, that he was on his way to pay him a visit. This he did in order to prevent any effect arising from an unexpected appearance. The king concluded that it was on account of the affair of Almeria, and that Cortes was enraged about that which in reality he did not care the value of a chesnut for, and sent back word to Cortes that he was welcome. Accordingly, our general, and we who attended him, having entered into the presence of Montezuma, after paying him his respects, he addressed the king through his interpreters, saying, he was astonished that a monarch who was so brave, and who had shewn himself so friendly to us, should have given orders to his troops in Tuzapan to attack the Spaniards, kill one of them, and his horse, and pillage and destroy our allies. Cortes wished to conceal the death of Escalante and the six others. He then charged the king with the treacherous attempt against us in Cholula, which he said he had hitherto been deterred from speaking of, by motives of esteem and regard; but that now, in addition to these provocations, his officers were plotting our immediate destruction, and he concluded by saying, that, in order to prevent the ruin of the city, it was necessary that his Majesty should, peaceably, and without making any opposition or remonstrance, immediately go with us to our quarters, where he should be treated with the greatest respect; but that if he said one word, or gave the least alarm, the five captains then present would instantly put him to death. On hearing this Montezuma was at first so terrified that he appeared to have lost all sensation. Having recovered himself a little, he denied his having ever given any order to his troops to attack our countrymen, and taking from his wrist the signet of Huitzilopochtli with which he was used to confirm any order of great importance, he caused the officer of whom complaint had been made, to be sent for. He then replied to the proposal of leaving his palace, and summoning up his dignity said, that he was not the person to be forced to take such a step, contrary to his inclination. The conversation was prolonged, Cortes giving him good reasons for what he proposed, and the king replying to him with better, insomuch that above half an hour had now elapsed. The captains who were standing by began at last to grow very impatient, and J. V. de Leon cried out to Cortes in his rough voice, "Why Sir do you waste so many words? Let him yield himself our prisoner, or we will this instant plunge our swords into his body. Tell him this, and also, that if he says a word, he dies for it. Better for us to assure our lives now, or perish at once." The manner in which this was spoken struck the king, and he asked Donna Marina the meaning of it. She with her usual readiness answered by requesting that he would immediately consent to what was proposed to him, and go where he should meet all respect and honor, as she perceived that if he hesitated, they were resolved to put him to instant death. He then addressed Cortes and said, "I have a legitimate son, and two legitimate daughters; take them as hostages for me, but do not expose me as a prisoner to my own people." Cortes however replied saying nothing but what was originally proposed could do, and that remonstrances were unavailing. At length he was forced to consent, upon which our captains addressed him with every declaration of esteem and respect, earnestly desiring that he would not be offended at what had passed, and that he would tell his officers and guards that he went by his own free will, and by the advice of his gods and priests. His magnificent state litters were now brought, and attended by his usual guards he proceeded to our quarters, where our posts and centinels being duly placed, he was received and entertained with every mark of respect. He was soon waited on by the princes of his family and the chief nobility of Mexico, who came to know the cause of the step that he had taken, and also if it was his wish that they should attack us; but he replied, that it was his intention to stay with us for a few days, and that whatever further commands he had for them, he would signify in due time; but charged them to do nothing to disturb the city.

# 11 / THE INTELLECTUAL MAYAS OF YUCATÁN, MEXICO

*The Mayas were not only the most intellectual of all the American Indian tribes and nations, but they surpassed all of the Old World peoples of antiquity as well in arithmetic, in astronomy, and in the accuracy of their calendar. They were well in advance of the Greeks and Romans, for instance, in these respects. They had a place numeral system with symbols for zero, comparable in general to our own "Arabic" system, except that the Maya assigned a value of 20 to each position instead of the 10 we use. If you don't think this principle is a significant advance over Roman numeral notation, try to do a problem in long division or to extract a square root in Roman numerals. The accuracy with which the Mayas measured the number of days in the solar year and in the cycles of the planet Venus has only been improved upon by the scientific astronomy of Europe in the last few centuries. Twelve hundred years ago the Mayas led the world in this knowledge. The weakness of the Mayan astronomical and calendrical achievement was its close association with their undemonstrable brand of astrology and mythology. The calendar was used principally to predict lucky and unlucky days in the future and to prophesy in some detail what was likely to happen. This confusion of fact and fiction made the Mayas an easy prey for the Spaniards, as it also did in the cases of the Aztecs and Incas.*

*Mayan civilization began about 400* B.C. *and reached its peak between* A.D. *625 and* A.D. *800. After* A.D. *800 less civilized but more*

Ralph L. Roys, *The Indian Background of Colonial Yucatán*, Carnegie Institution of Washington, Publication 548 (1943), pp. 13-22, 28-30, 33-35, 46, 49, 51-52, 65, 71-74, 76-77, 79-82, 84-91, 97.

*warlike peoples from central Mexico began to invade the land of the Mayas and reigned supreme during the Mexican period from* A.D. *975 to* A.D. *1200. Then followed the era when the city of Mayapán dominated all of Yucatán and the foreign ruling groups became acculturated to the Maya way of life. The kingdom of Mayapán collapsed about* A.D. *1450 and was broken up into the smaller independent states found by the Spanish in 1517.*

*Since Roys wrote, progress has been made in the decipherment of Mayan glyphs, but about half of them still defy the best brains in Mayan scholarship.*

When Francisco Hernandez de Cordoba discovered Yucatan in 1517, he found evidence of a new culture definitely superior to anything with which the Spaniards had previously met in the New World. His expedition appears to have landed first at Mujeres Island just off the northeast coast of the peninsula. . . .

At Cape Cotoche, a short distance farther north, they came to a town larger than any they had seen in the West Indies and which they named "Gran Cayro." . . . Out to the ships paddled a number of large dugout canoes, some of them holding as many as forty Indians, who were dressed in sleeveless jackets and loincloths. Their chief, making signs to the Spaniards to come ashore and visit his town, is said to have called to them *"conex cotoche,"* which means "Come to our houses." The newcomers took this to be the name of the site and called the cape Cotoche.

The invitation was accepted, although not without some misgivings, and the Spaniards even availed themselves of some of the native craft to go ashore. They went well provided with firearms and crossbows as well as swords and lances or pikes, but seem to have stopped and hesitated from time to time as they proceeded toward the town. The chief continued to press his invitation. Suddenly, as they approached a wooded spot, the chief gave a signal, and a body of warriors sprang from ambush and vigorously attacked them. This force was armed with bows and arrows, spears, slings, and the flint-edged wooden swords Columbus had already seen at Guanaja fifteen years before. They were protected with shields and quilted cotton armor. A number of the Spaniards were wounded and two of them afterward died; but the attacking party apparently was not a large one and was soon defeated with a loss of fifteen killed and two prisoners, whom the visitors carried off to serve as interpreters for a future occasion. . . .

Cordoba then sailed westward around the peninsula to Campeche, where the natives inquired by signs whether the Spaniards had come from the east and to the astonishment of the latter, pronounced the words "Castilan, Castilan." Bernal Diaz, who was present at the time, later associated this with the fact that two shipwrecked Spaniards had long been held captive on the east coast; but it seems equally probable that the name of the Spaniards had been carried, directly or indirectly, by native traders along the coast from Veragua, or perhaps from the Bay Islands. . . .

The impressions received by the Spaniards at Cotoche were further confirmed at Campeche. They were invited to come to the town and were conducted to some large temples of lime and stone, set on pyramids. Here an altar stained with blood showed signs of a recent human sacrifice; and they saw idols, figures of serpents, and fierce animals, and what appeared to be painted representations of crosses. The serpent was a well-known religious symbol found everywhere in the Maya and Mexican areas. The cross was a conventionalized tree, probably personified, and associated with rain ceremonies; in every wayside shrine today it is still painted green. The fierce animals may have been gods, but more likely they represented the Mexican military orders, which had been introduced into Yucatan. We find frequent reference to them in the Maya prophecies.

At first the chief seemed cordial, and some trading with the Indians ensued, during which the Spaniards are said to have acquired cotton mantles, featherwork, and objects of tortoise shell and gold. Later the attitude of the natives changed. Men dressed in shabby mantles, perhaps slaves, brought a quantity of dry reeds, and two companies of armed warriors stationed themselves near by. Then ten priests robed in long white mantles and carrying clay braziers of burning incense came out of a temple and indicated by signs that the reeds would be burned and the Spaniards must depart before they were consumed. The fire was lighted and the priests silently withdrew. The warriors began to sound their whistles, trumpets, and drums, and the Spaniards prudently left the scene and promptly embarked.

The next stop was at Champoton, where they landed to fill their water casks. Here armed natives quietly approached and by signs asked the same question as at Campeche. The Spaniards spent the night on shore, but by morning a large army of Indian warriors had assembled and began to attack them. The visitors stood their ground for a time, but the Indian forces were too great for them. Two were captured (and no doubt later sacrificed), fifty were killed, and almost all the remainder wounded, some of them mortally. The Spaniards retreated and embarked with difficulty, leaving their casks behind them.

These events of Cordoba's voyage will be familiar to most readers, but brief summary of them seems relevant here, since in our study of the Maya religion some attempt will be made to discuss the problem of the effect of the Kukulcan prophecies on the native attitude toward the Spaniards. As we shall see, the facts are confusing. Some of the Maya were evidently opportunists who hoped to turn the invasion to their own advantage; others were reluctant appeasers who temporized with the invaders; but there were many who, in spite of a certain supernatural awe in which the Spaniards were held, bitterly resisted them from first to last. . . .

It is difficult to escape the conclusion that many of the coast towns presented a very different appearance from those of the interior. We find many references to stone houses on the coast, but in the interior, except for the few contemporary temples of which we have any description, there is little indication that many buildings with stone walls were in actual use at the time, although abandoned vaulted structures were everywhere in evidence. To the Spaniards the culture of the coast in general seemed superior to that of the interior. . . .

Neither on the coast nor in the interior do the towns appear to have been regularly laid out in streets. This is specifically stated of the village of Zama and of such larger towns as Chauaca and Campeche. It is probable, however, that certain paved avenues in some towns led from the center to the outskirts, presumably to the ceremonial entrances of the town at the four cardinal points. . . .

The temples of the coast towns seem to have aroused more interest in the Spaniards than did those which they found in actual use in the interior. They were stepped pyramids, sometimes large, which were ascended by stone stairways and surmounted by small super-structures which the Spaniards called chapels. Many of these edifices had thatched roofs, but some, especially at Cozumel, are said to have been roofed with slabs of stone and were probably vaulted. . . .

The Spaniards were evidently less impressed by the contemporary architecture in the interior of Yucatan. Montejo, in an early letter to the Crown, has little to say of the temples and other buildings, but he writes: "The land is well populated with large cities and towns, very fresh [with verdure]; every town is an orchard of fruit trees." The newcomers were struck with the magnificence of the ancient monuments, few of which appear to have been in use at the time of the conquest. Uxmal was deserted, and I can find no record of any town still existing on the ground of the great ruined city of Izamal until the founding of the monastery there in 1552. The handsome remains at Merida were covered by a dense growth of forest, and Montejo found only a miserable village of thatched huts near the site. Although it is true that pilgrims still made sacri-fices at the Sacred Cenote [well] of Chichen Itza, the settlement there was small and the large edifices had greatly deteriorated.

A Maya town described by Landa is no doubt typical of the interior of the country, where he had traveled extensively before the Spaniards had time to effect many changes in the manner of living:

> Before the Spaniards had conquered that country, the natives lived together in towns in a very civilized fashion. They kept the land well cleared and free from weeds, and planted very good trees. Their dwelling place was as follows:—in the middle of the town were their temples with beautiful plazas, and all around the temples stood the houses of the lords and the priests, and then (those of) the most important people. Thus came the houses of the richest and of those who were held in the highest estimation nearest to these, and at the outskirts of the town were the houses of the lower class. And the wells, if there were but few of them, were near the houses of the lords; and they had their improved lands planted with wine trees and they sowed cotton, pepper and maize, and they lived thus close together for fear of their enemies, who took them captive, and it was owing to the wars of the Spaniards that they scattered in the woods. . . .

Although we have many early descriptions of the ancient temples at Merida, Uxmal, Izamal, and Chichen Itza, we find little in the early Spanish reports about those which were found in current use in the interior of the country. . . .

The contrast between the contemporary architecture of the interior and the imposing monuments of the past represents only one aspect of a change which had evidently been going on for some time. We shall note other evidences of it in the course of this study, as it formed an important part of the social and political background of the Yucatecan Maya. The ancient structures naturally aroused the curiosity of the Spaniards. Some of the Indians told them that they were the work of their own ancestors, while others ascribed them to foreigners whom the natives of the country had killed. A great revolution had occurred about the middle of the fifteenth century, resulting in the end of a centralized government and the destruction of its capital at Mayapan "the last notable city which the natives had." The country now broke up into a number of small independent states, which were constantly at war with one another. Mayapan was indeed a large fortified stone city, but its remains are so much less impressive than those of Uxmal, Chichen Itza, and other ancient centers of population, that one is tempted to believe that an architectural decline had already set in before its fall. It would appear, however, that if the coast towns also suffered from this decline, it was less marked than in the interior. . . .

Feasts and banquets played an important part in the life of the Maya. Some of these were public and religious, the entire town contributing to them. An intoxicating drink of fermented honey and water seasoned with certain bark or with roots was consumed in large quantities, and a saturnalia ensued. Drunkenness was general and was accompanied by brawling, destruction of property, and wild sexual excesses. Toward the end of the year one of the richest men of the town also gave a series of feasts at his home. These were apparently for the local nobility and were characterized by similar uproar and intoxication. We find this account of the festivals confirmed in the native prophecies, which suggest that the extravagant behavior was part of a religious pattern and not merely incidental to the general inebriation. One Maya narrative seems to ascribe the erotic features of these festivals to the introduction of the Kukulcan cult from Mexico. . . .

The kinds of dances were manifold; to one early Spanish observer it seemed as though there must be more than a thousand. Many, possibly most, had some religious significance. On one occasion all of 800 men were so engaged at a time. . . .

Dramatic representations, especially those given by professional performers, were mostly comedies. Sometimes they took place indoors and sometimes on open-air stages. Besides their usual entertainments at feasts and banquets, the comedians played an important part at the annual festival of Kukulcan, when they went about the town, performing at the principal houses and collecting offerings. They were graceful and witty and were very elegantly costumed. Often they wore masks and impersonated birds, making fun of the town magnates to their faces, but with old proverbs and veiled allusions. Indeed, they enjoyed the license of the European court jester. . . .

Yucatecan Maya society was definitely divided into three classes: nobles, commoners, and slaves. The Maya word for noble is *almehen* —derived from *al,* a woman's offspring, and *mehen,* a man's progeny —and thus the term implies known descent in both the male and female line. The nobles constituted the ruling class, filled the more important political offices, and were not only the most valiant warriors and members of the military orders but also the wealthiest farmers and merchants. Their economic advantage might well be ascribed partly to a certain preferred position in the use of the land and partly to their opportunities to exploit the labor of others, especially slaves, who were mostly captives taken in war. We know that many priests belonged to the nobility, as did probably the entire profession, so as holders of political office, military leaders, principal merchants, and clergy, the ruling class was able to control most fields of human activity. Nevertheless, except possibly for certain persons whose condition may have resembled serfdom, we have little evidence that the free plebeians generally had much reason to complain of oppression on the part of the nobles at the time of the conquest. . . .

The commoners made up the vast majority of the population. They comprised the free workers of the country, including the artisans, fishermen, and small farmers and merchants generally. . . .

There is some indication that below the ordinary commoners was a stratum of society, the members of which might be considered serfs, like the *mayeques* of Mexico. . . .

There were many slaves, most of them belonging to the nobles or wealthy commoners. The majority of them were men, women, and children of the plebeian class, who were captured in war. Noble prisoners were usually sacrificed, although they were sometimes ransomed. As we shall see, one of the principal causes of war was the desire to capture slaves. Others were seized for theft, especially in time of famine, and for unpaid damages at law, but their kin could always redeem them. Also a person who impregnated or married a slave was enslaved by the owner of the latter. A person could be born in servitude, but even then redemption was possible, and we find no evidence of breeding slaves for profit. . . .

According to the early Spanish writers the most important articles of commerce were salt, textiles, fish and copal incense. To these we might add pottery, flint implements, and certain objects of wood. There was also more or less sale or barter of other goods, but we gather from the various reports that they were largely produced by the consumer as needed. Except in some localities on or near the coast, like Chauacha and Zama, where little maize was grown, nearly everybody seems to have done some farming; and the producers of merchantable goods followed their callings at such times as work in the fields and necessary tasks about the home did not require their attention. A man might make many things for his own use but manufacture for sale only the one thing for the production of which he was specially trained or naturally adept. In the Motul dictionary a certain term is defined as "he who knows many crafts and he who is very proficient in some particular one." Here too we find the Maya names of a number of crafts or other occupations, such as carrier, charcoal-burner, dyer, farmer, fisherman, flint-worker, mason, painter or writer, potter, salt-gatherer, sandal-maker, stone-cutter, tanner and weaver. We suspect, indeed, that certain skilled craftsmen, whose products were much in demand, cultivated smaller milpas [farms] than the average person.

The textile industry was probably the most important. Everyone wore cotton clothing, practically every housewife spun and wove cotton, and the plant is said to have been cultivated almost everywhere. . . .

Landa tells us that since the Maya lacked metals,

> . . . God provided them with a ridge of flint near the range of hills, which . . . crosses the land, from which they got stones from which they made the heads of their lances for war and the knives for the sacrifices (of which the priests kept a good supply). They made the heads for their arrows and they still make them, and so flint served them for metal.

There was much commerce, both domestic and foreign, and trade was, as in Mexico, a highly honorable calling, especially when conducted on a large scale. The son of the last Cocom ruler at Mayapan was in Honduras on a trading expedition at the time of the fall of that city. Merchants ranged from the wealthy and noble wholesalers, who had their own factors, trading canoes, and slave carriers, to the petty itinerant who carried his own pack. Once there had been wide causeways across the country, leading to certain centers of pilgrimage, but at the time of the conquest they were completely a thing of the past and had probably not been used for centuries. The highways of commerce were then rough narrow trails through the thick bush, the overhanging branches cut high enough just to clear a man's head and pack. Needless to say, the mounted Spaniards found them difficult to travel. . . .

The principal media of exchange were cacao beans, beads of red shell, jade, and other green stones, small copper hatchets, and bells like sleigh bells. Cacao and shell beads came the nearest to taking the place of money. . . .

If we take into consideration the historical background of northern Yucatan, it is not surprising that the independent states, into which the Spaniards found the country divided, were constantly at war with one another. As we have seen, each so-called province was under the control of an aristocratic caste. Most, if not all, of its members believed themselves to be descended from the warlike Mexican adventurers, who had entered and dominated the country several centuries before; but this does not seem to have deterred them from making war on one another. This ruling class had, generally speaking, adopted most of the customs of the autochthonous population, and they all spoke its language, although they retained to some extent the religion and warlike traditions of the early invaders. Captives taken in war were desirable for sacrifice, but we may well infer from the reliefs on the older monuments that his was by no means a foreign innovation. Caciques [chiefs] and other leading men kept many slaves, and this supply of labor was recruited largely by means of warfare. It was the policy of each state to exploit its own commerce, as far as possible, at the expense of its neighbors. Finally, as we have already seen, the agricultural system involved letting the land revert to forest for a considerable number of years after two consecutive seasons in crop. This offered a temptation to an aggressive group of people living near a frontier to trespass across the boundary, cut the forest, and grow and harvest a crop, before the authorities of the neighboring province would be ready to interfere, particularly since it was not customary to make war during the growing season. With such agricultural conditions a considerable proportion of the population thus tended to live in scattered hamlets. . . .

The religious beliefs and practices of the Maya were an important factor in the attitude of the Spaniards and natives toward one another from the very first and continued to affect their subsequent relations. The two races were impressed by the striking, if superficial, resemblances in their religious rites. Crosses, altars, and incense were sacred to both; confession of sin, baptism of children, fasting, continence, and the ceremonial consumption of fermented liquor were common practices.

One of the first things to arrest the attention of the Spaniards who navigated the coast of Yucatan was the religious architecture. They were enormously impressed by the large stone pyramid temples; and it is evident from the records of the early expeditions that they displayed considerable interest in what they found inside these buildings. Except on the Island of Cozumel, the first explorers tell little of conditions within the towns, but on Cape Catoche and at Campeche and Champoton they found temples by the seashore, evidently devoted to the worship of the gods of the fishermen and hunters of aquatic fowl. Similar shrines on Laguna de Terminos were also visited by traveling merchants, who doubtless frequented those on the Yucatan coast. . . .

The Maya cosmos, like that of the Mexicans, seems to have consisted of thirteen heavens and nine hells. In the native literature we frequently read of a group of thirteen gods called Oxlahun-ti-ku and another of nine gods known as Bolon-ti-ku. They are evidently the deities of the thirteen heavens and nine hells, especially since the Bolon-ti-ku appear to be of a malevolent character. We can not identify the members of these groups, but it seems probable that the sky god, Itzamna, was chief of the former, and that such deities as Cumhau "the prince of devils," and the death god, Uac-mitun-ahau, were prominent among the latter. . . .

At the time of the conquest the head of the Yucatecan Maya pantheon was the sky god, Itzamna. *Itzam* means a large land or water lizard, and the name might perhaps be translated as "house of the lizard." The association is confirmed by the Maya symbol for the sky, which is a lizard monster with astronomical signs on its long snakelike body, and a face, apparently that of the god himself, seems to look forth from between the jaws of another lizard monster, which, however, lacks the astronomical symbols. The god has the face of an old man with a Roman nose and an almost toothless mouth. One source makes Itzamna the son of Kinich Ahau ("sun-eyed or sun-faced lord"), the sun god, whereas two others state that he was formerly a man. All agree that he was the inventor of writing. Itzamna and Kinich Ahau are given as names of the same personage, and the faces of these two gods resemble one another, although the latter can usually be distinguished by a curved symbol over the nose. It seems likely that both represented different aspects of the same deity. Itzamna was the great food-giver, and in this aspect he was often called Itzamna Kauil, since *kauil* is a word for food. In times of drought and famine they prayed to him, along with the rain gods, to send rain for the crops. As the first priest and inventor of writing, he was also one of the gods of medicine and invoked as Kinich Ahau Itzamna at a special festival of priests, medicine men, and magicians, when they ritually cleansed their books and read the prophecy for the coming year.

As already explained, Maya culture was founded on agriculture. When the crops failed and any surplus food had been consumed, the people scattered to the forests to eke out a miserable existence on such wild fruits, roots, and game as could be found, and chaos prevailed until the rains came again and the orderly course of civilized life could be resumed. Consequently the daily religion of the rank and file of the population centered around the rain and wind gods, on whose favor the crops depended. These were the deities who were, and still are, invoked when the bush is cut and burned, the fields are planted, and the grain is growing. Today, in addition to their other names, they are called the guardians of the forest, of the fertile wild lands, and of the fields; and it seems probable that these or other very similar appellations have always expressed the popular conception of the agricultural gods. Forest and field are closely related, since the forest of one year is the cultivated field of the next. . . .

Class distinctions in Yucatan sometimes extended even to religion, for we are told that every cacique or principal who had Indians subject to him had certain gods, whom the common people were not allowed to worship directly. If the latter wished to make offerings to these deities, they must do it through their lord. There can be little doubt that we have here gods introduced by the Mexican invaders. Chief among them was Kukulcan, the quetzal serpent, whose Maya name is simply a translation of Quetzalcoatl [plumed serpent], the well-known Mexican culture hero. The Maya explained him as a Mexican captain, a great lord who came with his followers from foreign parts to Yucatan and taught the people to practice idolatry. . . .

This deity was connected in a way with the Spanish conquest. Just as the return of Quetzalcoatl from the east was foretold in Mexico, so in Yucatan there was a definite prophecy that he would one day come back to that country with the Itza. When the Spaniards appeared from that quarter bearing the cross, which so startlingly resembled one of the most sacred Maya symbols, there can be little doubt that many of the natives were enormously impressed. If the first Spaniards met with an unfriendly reception by some of the Yucatecan states, the same occurred to Cortez in Mexico, and yet we know that the Quetzalcoatl myth had an important influence on Montezuma's attitude toward the invaders. The Maya literature of the colonial period compares the Spanish invasion with that of the Itza, and to the native mind it must have seemed more than a coincidence that Montejo's first attempt to establish himself was at the old Itza capital associated with Kukulcan. If this effort was unsuccessful, the same was believed to have been true of the first Itza occupation of that site. It must be remembered also that the fulfillment of the prophecy was not generally desired by a great part of the native population; the Itza were remembered with anything but kindly feelings in much of northern Yucatan. . . .

A priest who performed human sacrifices was called a nacom, the same title that was applied to the war chief. Evidently a chilan [diviner] could fill this position, for the famous prophet Chilam Balam, was also called Nacom Balam. Landa tells us that the office of nacom was not considered very honorable, but this is evidently an error, for in postconquest times, when the religious organization had more or less broken down, we find caciques and other important men performing this service. Finally there were four old men called chacs, who were appointed each year from the laity to assist in sacrifices and other ceremonies.

Although cotton vestments were sometimes worn, the usual costume of the priests was a long white sleeveless robe of bark cloth, the skirt often ornamented with snail shells. The headdress was a miterlike crown similar in form to that worn by the Mexican rulers and seen on some of the warlike figures dating from the Mexican period in the reliefs at Chichen Itza. The hair was unkempt and smeared with sacrificial blood. The shells and pointed crown recall the representations of Quetzalcoatl and strongly suggest a Mexican origin for this costume. The unkempt hair smeared with blood was typical also of the Mexican priesthood. During baptismal ceremonies the priest wore a short red jacket of feather mosaic work with long feathers trailing from its edge, and on his head a crown of feathers.

The principal functions of the priests were to propitiate the gods and keep track of the calendar, telling the people when to celebrate religious festivals and when to burn and plant their fields, hunt, or go to war. They also officiated at various domestic ceremonies such as weddings, baptisms, and confession; and they preached sermons and enforced religious observances. In punishing religious delinquency they are said to have had more authority than the temporal rulers. Although Landa refers to the baptism of very young children, other sources seem to indicate that it may have been a puberty ceremony. As in the Christian religion, it was called "rebirth" (*caput zihil*). . . .

Of the various rites perhaps the most important were those in honor of the new year; these began during the last five days of the old. The gods of the four cardinal points presided in turn over the year ascribed to their own world quarter. Elaborate formalities were observed in dismissing the old incumbents and installing the new in office. They took place at the temple, at the four entrances to the town, and in the private oratory of the patron of the festival. Human sacrifice was sometimes performed at the inauguration of the east year, and at that of the south year a spectacular fire-walking rite took place. There was a great dance, and a structure was built of bundles of faggots in the temple court. This was set on fire, and the burning coals were leveled off; then a priest dressed in his ceremonial bark-cloth robe and miter, singing and bearing an idol, passed over the fire barefoot and unscathed, sprinkling the coals with an aspergill of snakes' tails. He was accompanied by the dancers, some of whom suffered severely from burns, especially if they were unduly intoxicated. . . .

At some festivals human sacrifice was required, but more often animals and other offerings were sufficient, human victims being considered necessary only in time of public calamity, to avert drought and famine, to prevent the recurrence of a hurricane, or to prolong the life of a sick ruler. On ordinary occasions, when people prayed for rain, abundant crops, health, good hunting or fishing, and success in war, the clergy and laity alike offered their own blood, drawn from the ear, lip, tongue, and various parts of the body. There were also sacrifices of turkeys, dogs, and various wild animals, birds, and sometimes reptiles, as well as oblations of food, feathers, and precious stones. Copal resin was burned on all occasions and sometimes chicle, the gum of the rubber tree, or that of a species of Notoptera. Women prepared food offerings and sometimes burned incense, but they did not make sacrifices; and only on very rare occasions were certain old women admitted to the temple ceremonies.

With human sacrifice a certain sense of proportion was observed and it never became as common as in the highlands of Mexico.

The victims were war prisoners of rank, slave men and women, including the humbler captives and persons enslaved for theft or some other crime, for whose purchase the community contributed funds, and finally many children. The last, as in Mexico, were especially acceptable to the agricultural deities. Of these many were purchased from neighboring towns or provinces, and during the two decades immediately following the Spanish conquest it was so customary to kidnap children from other districts for this purpose that it seems reasonable to ascribe the practice to pre-Spanish times as well. Gifts of children for sacrifice were also sent from one ruler to another. Men are said to have piously donated their own children at times, but from the instances cited in Landa's inquisition proceedings in 1562, it seems more likely that these were usually either their offspring by female slaves or orphaned relatives reared by wealthy men. In many cases persons designated for sacrifice were kept in wooden cages.

In front of the stairway in the temple court was a round stone dais with steps and on it a sacrificial stone four or five spans high. There was also a similar stone at the top of the pyramid in front of the temple cell. The victim's body was painted blue, a paper crown placed upon his head, and he was stretched on his back over the stone. His arms and legs were held by the four chacs, while the nacom excised his heart with a large flint knife, which was called the hand or arm of god. The heart was placed in a shallow covered bowl and given to the priest, who offered it to the idols inside the temple and smeared their mouths with the blood. Later the heart was often burned in the same receptacle. On a certain occasion, when the sacrifice was performed at the top of the pyramid, the body was thrown down the steep steps and flayed. A priest then put on the skin and danced in it, after which ceremonial cannibalism sometimes ensued; but more often the body was buried in the temple court. This was evidently an importation from Mexico, where a similar sacrifice was made to Xipe Totec, originally a maize god. The flaying of the victim is believed to have symbolized the husking of the corn. . . .

Volumes have been written about the intellectual achievements of the Maya, and indeed we have ample evidence that their knowledge of mathematics, chronology, and astronomy was truly amazing.

In many inscriptions and at least one of the hieroglyphic codices we find a day count, which goes back to a mythical era some 4000 years before the latest date recorded by this system. The current moon age is often given, together with the position of the last completed lunation in a lunar year of five or six months. Arithmetical calculations are frequently found involving many thousands of days, some of them running into millions; and evidence has been adduced to show the existence of corrective formulas, by which the 365-day Maya calendar year was kept in harmony with the 365.24-day tropical year. The Dresden Codex contains a set of tables covering the synodical revolutions of the planet Venus during more than three centuries; and in the same manuscript is another table recording successive lunations in groups of five or six moons each for a period of nearly thirty-three years. The latter is apparently a table of eclipse syzygies, and, whether or not the Maya were able to predict eclipses, they appear to have known when one was likely to occur. Perhaps the greatest mathematical achievement of the Maya was their independent discovery of numeral place-value notation and the use of a zero, which must have greatly facilitated their chronological and astronomical calculations.

The inscriptions and codex which are the sources of a large part of this information, however, antedate the Spanish conquest by several centuries at least. There are some indications that the decadence of Maya architecture, which we have already noted, was accompanied by an intellectual decline; and it is impossible to say how much of this scientific knowledge still existed at the time of the conquest. Certainly, if it still survived, a great deal of it escaped the notice of the Spanish missionaries and settlers. The long day count, which for centuries was the framework for recording astronomical observations, had apparently fallen into disuse; and according to a colonial Maya manuscript certain foreigners, the Itza, had brought to an end a golden age, when everybody was happy, healthy, and good, when "in due measure did they recite the good prayers; in due measure they sought the lucky days, until they saw the good stars enter into their reign; then they kept watch while the reign of the good stars began."

On the other hand, hieroglyphic writing was still in use, and the complicated calendar still functioned. The priests kept track of the calendar and informed the people when to prepare to burn and plant their fields, which would imply that they were able to compute the variation of the 365-day Maya year from the true solar year. Moreover the survival of the Dresden Codex suggests that a few erudite persons at least still understood the chronological calculations and astronomical tables which it contains.

Most of the Maya sciences were based on the calendar, which was a combination of three different day counts. The first was a ritual period of 260 days made up of twenty day names combined with the numbers 1 to 13 as coefficients. Names and numbers followed one another without interruption, and, since the least common multiple of 20 and 13 is 260, the same day and coefficient recurred every 260 days. Then there was a 365-day year composed of eighteen months of twenty days each, with a special period of five unlucky days added at the end. The number of the day of the month and the name of the month fixed the day within this year; but this position fell a day short of the agricultural season by nearly a day every four years, since there were no leap years. In the colonial Maya manuscripts the year itself is often designated by the name and coefficient of its first day, a device which may have been borrowed from Mexico, since it is rarely employed, if at all, in the older Maya inscriptions. A day was often designated by its name and coefficient followed by its position in the 365-day year; but this fixed it only within a cycle of fifty-two such years known as a Calendar Round. Additional information was needed to place it more definitely.

Longer periods of time, however, were not reckoned in terms of the 365-day year, but by a chronological year of 360 days called a *tun*. Each tun was divided into eighteen *uinals* of twenty days each, and twenty tuns constituted a *katun* of 7200 days, or nearly twenty solar years. In the old Long Count already mentioned we also find a period of twenty katuns, or 144,000 days, which modern scholars call a cycle, or *baktun;* but this period was unknown to the sixteenth-century Spanish writers, and only in a single instance have I found an apparent reference to it in a colonial Maya manuscript.

At the time of the conquest the usual method of dating events appears to have been less precise, judged by the native books of the colonial period. Here the time of an event is often indicated by giving only the name and coefficient of the last day of the katun in which it occurred. The actual name of this closing day is always the same, Ahau, and only the coefficient varies; but for convenience I shall call the combination of day name and coefficient the name of the katun. Since a katun of the same name could recur only every thirteen katuns, or approximately 256 years, an indication of this sort places the event some time in a given katun but does not tell us in which katun round it occurred. The last must be determined in some other manner. An attempt to accomplish this has been made in most of the Maya chronicles by setting down a number of katun rounds, one after the other. These chronicles are of enormous historical value; but they were evidently compiled after the end of the sixteenth century, and there are indications that the native chroniclers sometimes confused the sequence of the katun rounds.

Since some religious ceremonies or festivals were determined by their position in the 260-day period, others were decided on their place in the 365-day year, and still others were celebrated at the beginning, middle, or end of the 7200-day katun, it is obvious that the priest, whose duty it was to announce the approach of these important occasions and prepare for them, must have had a considerable knowledge of arithmetic.

For counting objects the Maya employed the vigesimal system so common among primitive peoples, the ascending units most commonly used being 1 (*hun*), 20 (*kal*), 400 (*bak*), and 8000 (*pic*). The Spaniards were impressed with the facility and rapidity with which people counted cacao beans; cacao was not sold by dry measure or weight, but by counting each kernel, possibly in order to detect the substitution of an inferior species or of imitation kernels. It was sold in 400-kernel lots and probably in quantities of 8000 also, as we know was the case in Tabasco. The latter amount presumably constituted a load. Father Beltran in his Maya grammar also mentions three higher ascending units. The first was one *calab*, or 160,000. The second was one *kinchil*, or *tzotzceh*, which he defines as 1,000,000; but it probably meant 3,200,000, since the next higher order was the *alau*, which he tells us equaled 64,000,000. . . .

For counting either objects or days, numbers under twenty were recorded by dots up to four, and by bars, each of which signified five. Nineteen, for example, would be three bars and four dots.

Landa states that they made their counts "on the ground or on something smooth." Thompson suggests that counters may have been used, such as grains of maize, beans, or pebbles, and a short stick or bean pod could have taken the place of the bar. In the calendrical computations the day, uinal, tun, katun, and cycle are indicated either by glyphs or by their positions in ascending columns. . . .

The real character of Maya writing still remains somewhat debatable. As yet it has been possible to decipher with certainty only those glyphs which have a numerical, calendrical, or astronomical significance. Some other characters appear to designate certain deities and possibly a few of the objects depicted in the illustrations accompanying the hieroglyphic texts in the codices. The glyphs seem to be chiefly ideographic but contain a phonetic element, apparently including rebus forms.

The knowledge of this writing was confined to the priesthood and some members of the nobility, although the latter made no public use of the accomplishment. Since we are told that the priests were members of the aristocracy and not commoners, the principal key to Maya science was apparently in the hands of a ruling class of allegedly foreign origin. Their books were made of bark paper from a species of Ficus, possibly *F. cotinifolia,* and covered with a smooth lime sizing, on which glyphs and pictorial illustrations were painted in various colors. A long sheet of this paper was folded like a screen between two boards, so that it resembled a bound volume.

Only three Maya hieroglyphic manuscripts have come down to us. Of these one was purchased in Austria for the Royal Public Library at Dresden; another, the Tro-Cortesianus, is really one codex composed of two parts discovered separately in Spain; and the third, called the Peresianus, was found in the Imperial Library at Paris wrapped in a paper on which the name Perez was written. We have not the slightest information regarding their origin or how they came to be brought to Europe; and no Maya codex has as yet been found in America, although there is evidence that some still existed in Yucatan at the end of the seventeenth century. The Dresden Codex is apparently the oldest and has been thought to date from about A.D. 1100. Besides the dates and chronological computations already discussed, it deals sometimes with ceremonies of the 365-day year but more often with the 260-day period. These portions of the book are believed to be a religious and astrological almanac and concerned with ceremonies, rituals, and offerings, as well as showing the lucky or unlucky days for the various activities of life. The Codex Tro-Cortesianus is devoted almost entirely to the 260-day period. The third, the Codex Peresianus, although it treats of the Maya zodiac and much of it is astronomical and chronological, may possibly contain some prophetic material.

Strangely enough, the Maya did not employ their graphic system to write letters or contracts, and lawsuits were settled entirely by word of mouth; nevertheless, their hieroglyphic literature seems to have covered nearly every branch of Maya science. Landa writes:

> The sciences which they taught were computations of the years, months, and days, the festivals and ceremonies, the administration of the sacraments, the fateful days and seasons, their methods of divination and their prophecies, events and cures for diseases, and their antiquities and how to read and write with the letters and characters with which they wrote, and drawings which illustrate the meaning of the writings.

In another passage he tells us that genealogy was also one of their sciences.

Their "computations of the years, months, and days" are amply confirmed by the inscriptions and hieroglyphic codices that are extant. That these manuscripts also dealt with "the festivals and ceremonies" as well as "the administration of the sacraments" seems evident from the pictures accompanying the texts. What appears to be a survival of this type of literature is found in the so-called Books of Chilam Balam, written in Maya but with European script. Here we see native almanacs, which continued to be used throughout the eighteenth century and probably even later. Although not entirely correct, these are mostly correlations of the Christian annual calendar with the Maya months and the 260-day period. Each day of the latter is designated as good or bad; some are also declared to be suitable for planting certain crops, hunting, hiving bees, or other undertakings. A number of them are specified as lucky or unlucky for certain professions or classes of persons; others are apt to bring disease. Accompanying these prognostics are occasional weather predictions and a few obscurely worded phrases which may refer to pagan ceremonies. Toward the end of the colonial period the names of the saints are added, and these native books tend more and more to resemble the contemporary Spanish almanacs; but in the Codex Perez is a fragment of an earlier form, in which all reference to the Christian calendar is omitted. Here the glyph of the day name is followed by its name, coefficient, and prediction written out in European script.

Of special interest are the prophecies of the katuns, which also appear in the Books of Chilam Balam. As we have already seen, these time periods were of nearly twenty years each, and in every thirteen katuns one of the same name came around again. The principal basis of these prophecies was the belief that whatever had happened in the past would be likely to recur in another katun of the same name. Consequently these prophecies are full of historical allusions, although unfortunately we are not told in which series of katuns the events occurred.

Some of the prognostics are auspicious, but a surprisingly large number of them are unfavorable. War, pestilence, drought, locusts, famine, riot, and political upheaval are freely predicted, during which the people will be obliged to leave their homes and find their food in the forests. Some misfortunes seem to be symbolized by the deities who brought them; and certain events are indicated by simply naming a prominent person or a place associated with the occurrence. . . .

Many of the Spanish chroniclers tell us that the Maya wrote down their history in their hieroglyphic manuscripts, but the precise character of these records of past events is difficult to determine. As we have already seen, in four of the Maya chronicles a number of successive katun rounds are set down, and opposite the names of some katuns are historical entries, the times of which are implied by their positions in this long series. . . .

It also seems very possible that many of the histories in hieroglyphic writing, to which the Spanish writers refer, were simply the katun prophecies with their historical allusions. History and prophecy were evidently closely associated in people's minds.

As already noted, few glyphs except those concerning numbers, the calendar, or astronomical phenomena have been satisfactorily interpreted; and, although the undeciphered glyphs in the surviving codices remain more or less a matter of conjecture, they hardly seem to be sufficiently numerous to cover the large variety of subject matter, which reliable writers of the sixteenth and seventeenth centuries tell us was set down in hieroglyphics. There are two possible explanations which might account for this. One is the character of the Maya language. Not only do many homonyms appear in the older dictionaries, but, by various associations of ideas, a single root with its derivations is frequently expanded so that it may convey a very considerable number of different meanings. This suggests the possibility that the same glyph may have expressed a variety of ideas. The other is the limited range of subjects treated in the few Maya codices that we have. As we have seen, these appear to be confined to ceremonial, chronological, and astronomical treatises; and it seems not unlikely that, if we had any of the manuscripts dealing with other matters, such as past events, prophecy, or the healing art, they would be found to contain a wider variety of hieroglyphic symbols.

# CONCLUSION

## INDIAN RECEPTION AND RESISTANCE TO EUROPEANS

The European cultures that colonized the Americas encountered varying degrees of reception and resistance from the Indians they contacted. This was due to the differences in the colonizing policies and practices of European nations as well as to the many differences among the Indian cultures in the New World.

The avowed purpose of the first voyage of Christopher Columbus was to discover a new route to the Far East which would be shorter and easier to negotiate than that around the Cape of Good Hope in Africa. Such a route would have given the Spanish an advantage in the trade with the East and would have increased the wealth of their royalty and upper classes. The Spanish had no desire at first to establish a new nation with new ideals, but were content to enhance the wealth and prestige of their current nation and its vested interests. The Spaniard in the lower ranks hoped to gain favor in the eyes of his upper-class sponsor and to earn a fortune large enough to permit a speedy return to Spain and a life of leisure there.

After the Spanish realized that they had discovered new continents teeming with millions of unsaved souls, their colonization included a religious crusade to Christianize the masses in the New World. The "Christian Kings," Ferdinand and Isabella, fresh from their victory over the Moors, wished to spread Christianity to their new kingdoms across the seas. They and their devout successors,

156

Charles V and Philip II, sent many Dominicans, Franciscans, and later, Jesuits to the Americas for this purpose; and even their military representatives conquered the Indians in the name of their God and King. The French also sent many Jesuits to Canada and to the Mississippi Valley in the seventeenth century, and Jesuits and other priests followed the Portuguese flag in Brazil.

In the sixteenth century the purposes of English exploration in the hands of adventurous men, such as Sir Francis Drake, differed little from those of the Spanish; but the seventeenth century witnessed the settling of New England and the Middle Atlantic states by religious idealists from the middle and lower classes, such as the Puritans and Quakers. These people were so busy establishing their own independence from Roman Catholicism that they did not begin missionary work among Indians until well into the eighteenth century.

Luckily for the Spanish, they encountered the wealthiest Indians in the New World in Mexico and Peru. They promptly defeated them in war, robbed them of their gold and other valuables, deposed their political leaders, appointed Spaniards in their places, and proceeded to operate these colonies according to the feudal system of Spain. Largely because the Indians of Mexico and Peru had paid taxes and taken orders from overlords of some kind literally from time immemorial, they knew no model for rebellion and yielded to the iron hand of the Spaniards. The population in these areas was so large and dense that it was impossible for most of the Indians to flee to some place of refuge. Another thing which helped the Spanish to regiment the Indian was the latter's habit of daily work, at farming, mining, crafts, and on public works, which had been going on for centuries before the Spanish arrived. Indian men did most of the farm work and all other labor away from home, while the women performed household tasks and sometimes wove cloth or made pottery vessels. Men accustomed to daily work will submit to forced labor or excessive taxation much more readily than those who habitually only hunt and fight.

The principal farm products exported from the Spanish colonies were sugar, cowhides, tobacco, cotton, and chocolate. In addition to these the Indians raised quantities of wheat and wine grapes for the consumption of their landlords, and continued to raise corn and other native American domesticated plants for their own subsistence. In New England and the North Atlantic states the colonists were looking for unoccupied land on which to live a freer and economically fuller life unfettered by English class structure. They had no desire to enslave or enserf Indians to work for them, and whatever attempts they may have made to encourage Indian men to settle down and farm English style failed because the Indians in these areas regarded the cultivation of the soil as women's work. Indian women had done most of the farm work in the eastern United States for centuries before Europeans arrived. In the beginning the men of these tribes obtained furs for the English colonists and acquired firearms and metal tools in exchange. This inevitably reduced the game to the point where the Indians were willing to sell their land and fight their way west to live in territory previously controlled by other tribes. The process included outbursts of violence against the Whites who had indirectly caused the trouble, followed by defeat of the Indians with a treaty and the ceding of even more land to the conquerers. In this way the Indians were either killed locally by disease, malnutrition, or violence, or were forced to move west where conflicts with other tribes produced a high mortality. The Indians in the western half of the United States lasted longer because they were farther from the colonists on the Atlantic Coast. Those on the Great Plains experienced a brief period of seeming prosperity from about 1800 to 1850, when the horse, the gun, and the demand for buffalo hides stepped up their economy. But this bubble burst in the last half of the nineteenth century and the survivors ended up on reservations.

In Canada, Indians have fared much better and have continued to trap furs to this day without severe loss of land or population. They were even farther removed from areas of large White population.

Around the Caribbean the Spanish attempted to put the men to work on plantations, but here, as on the east coast of what is now the United States, the Indians failed to respond and, from the middle of the sixteenth century, Negro slaves constituted the bulk of the laboring population. Most of the Indians died from European diseases, forced labor, violence, and malnutrition within a century of Columbus's first contact, but a few crossbred with the Spanish, became acculturated to the Spanish language and behavior, thus becoming absorbed into the Spanish population.

In the Marginal (nonfarming) culture area in southern Argentina and in southern Chile, the Indians failed to fit into the Spanish system, but they enjoyed independence for a short time after they formed predatory bands of horse nomads. Later these Indians became absorbed racially, linguistically, and culturally into the rural proletariat known as the "Gauchos of Argentina." The Tierra del Fuegians are now virtually extinct and have never made a significant contribution to post-Columbian economy.

The Spanish and English in the New World differed in another respect. About 90 per cent of the Spanish colonists were single men desirous of making a quick fortune and returning to Spain. Those who failed to do this stayed on in America, cohabiting with and marrying Indian women and producing Mestizo offspring. Most of the Englishmen, on the other hand, brought wives along with them or married English women at a later date in the colonies.

In the Spanish colonies as a whole the number of Spaniards never exceeded 5 per cent of the total population, while in the thirteen English colonies the Indians were outnumbered as early as about 1700. At the time of our Revolutionary War the number of Europeans in the thirteen colonies was greater than that of Indians in the entire area of what is now the United States.

A comparison of Indian population trends in the United States and Mexico is enlightening. In the United States, Indian population dropped from an estimated 2,000,000 in A.D. 1600 to about 200,000 in A.D. 1900, a reduction to 10 per cent in three centuries. Since that time it has risen steadily. In the southern half of Mexico, Indian population dropped from a high of 11,000,000 to 30,000,000 in A.D. 1519 to a low of 1,500,000 in A.D. 1650; a reduction to between 5 and 14 per cent in a century and a half. After A.D. 1650 it gradually began to rise, however. The Spanish need for the Indian as cheap labor in their colonial system did not prevent a mortality rate about the same as that in the United States, where Whites were openly hostile toward Indians and sometimes shot them on sight. The essential difference was in the time involved. The Spanish system in Mexico was more deadly in the beginning, when European diseases, malnutrition, forced labor, and violence took their toll, but it improved after A.D. 1650. Our system in the United States was more gradual and took three centuries to run its course.

In the 1960 census our Indians numbered about 500,000, a quarter of one per cent of the total U.S.A. population. In Mexico in 1960 no racial distinctions were made in the census, but it is estimated that about 80 per cent of the genes in the population were of Indian origin. The other 20 per cent were about equally divided between Spanish and Negro sources. In Guatemala the percentage of Indian genes might be even higher than that in Mexico, and in Ecuador, Peru, and Bolivia the percentage would not be far from the Mexican figure.

The Portuguese established a feudal system on the coast of Brazil in the sixteenth century, but the Indian men, such as those of the Tupinamba, were poor workers because they had been accustomed to letting the women farm while they hunted and fought, as in the eastern United States. The Portuguese attempted to enslave the Indians and conducted brutal slave hunts to obtain new workers when the old ones died, also of disease, malnutrition, and violence, or fled the plantation. The result was that most of the Indians on the coast disappeared in a few decades and Negro slaves had to be imported to work on the sugar plantations. This experience parallels that of the Spanish in the Caribbean.

The Colonial efforts of the Spanish in New Mexico among peoples like the Zuñi in the seventeenth century produced much less spectacular results than those in Mexico and Peru in the sixteenth century. Although the Pueblo men were accustomed to doing the farm work, and farm products constituted 75 or 80 per cent of the diet, each man farmed for himself and his family, not for some overlord. The total absence of hereditary class structure and the extreme smallness of the Indian political unit made it difficult for the Spanish to get much of economic value from the Indian. There was no huge established governmental hierarchy for the Spanish to take over, as there was in Mexico and Peru. Nevertheless the Spaniards put the Indians to work weaving blankets and cloth and gathering pine nuts, and they exported these items to Mexico, instead of the gold and silver they had hoped to find.

The Spanish attempt to civilize and regiment the Chichimecs of northeast Mexico was one of their biggest failures. There were few furs or other natural resources which the Indians could hunt or collect for the Spanish in that area; and the Indians refused to settle down and farm. The result was the annihilation of most of the Indian population in two centuries of wars.

In the Arctic the Eskimos obtained furs and ivory for the Russians, English, and Danes, but the quantity was not as great as in the interior of Canada and Alaska. On the Northwest Coast of North America furs were also the most profitable trade item received by the Russians and the English from the Indians. Hunting had been the principal occupation of men in these regions for thousands of years; so they responded readily to the European and Asian demand for furs.

With respect to religion, we may compare the success and failure of the various European powers in Christianizing the Indians. In terms of sheer numbers of nominal converts, the Spanish far outdistanced the English. The reasons for this are not hard to find: native population in Latin America was ten to twenty times as heavy as it was in Anglo-America; Roman Catholic ritual, with its elaborate costumes and pageantry, appealed to the Indians because it was much more like that of the complex Indian religions in Mexico and Peru than was the more bland Protestant service; the Roman Catholic priests permitted the Indians to retain many of their aboriginal beliefs and rituals, which would have been intolerable to Protestants; and the Spanish began the missionary work more than two centuries earlier than the English. The Catholic priests also sometimes baptized thousands of Indians in a single day, even though most of them knew no Spanish and had not the vaguest notion of what the new religion was all about. The more demanding requisites for membership in the Protestant sects ruled out such mass production of converts.

The Catholic clergy of the Spanish, on the whole, was as extreme in its concern for the welfare of the Indians as were the military and political factions in their disregard of it. The priests made every effort to stop the inhumane treatment of the Indians that they witnessed at every turn, but with relatively little success. Even in areas where the primary purpose of the colonization was to Christianize the Indians, as it was on the coast of California from 1769 to 1830, the score at the end showed that the souls of the natives had been saved at the expense of their bodies. The Indian population in the Mission Strip was reduced from 54,000 to 18,000 after only sixty-one years of exposure to the Spanish. The causes of death were the same as in other areas: European diseases, malnutrition, forced labor, and violence.

With respect to language, the many Indian languages in Latin America had more influence on Spanish than did Anglo-American Indian languages on English. The proof of this is the huge three-volume *Diccionario General de Americanismos,* by Francisco J. Santa María, which gives tens of thousands of words added to the Spanish of Latin America. Most such words are of Indian origin. There is no comparable Indian-English dictionary. This difference is easily explained by the small minority (5 per cent or fewer) of Spanish immigrants in Spain's colonies and the large majority of Indians who knew no Spanish in the beginning. Spaniards were forced to learn Indian words in order to communicate with the Indians who worked for them. However, in both Anglo-America and Latin America there are thousands of Indian geographical names for rivers, mountains, lakes, etc., which no scholar has yet attempted to assemble. Although almost everyone in Latin America speaks Spanish or Portuguese today, the number still speaking Indian languages totals at least ten million. The majority of these are bilingual; that is, they speak both an Indian language and Spanish or Portuguese. In Anglo-America only about one half million speak Indian languages and most of these double in English. The largest tribe in the United States in 1960 was the Navaho, estimated at eighty thousand, all of whom still speak Navaho, although most also know English.

The superiority of Anglo-America over much of Latin America today in its system of government, in technology, and in the health, education, and welfare of its population, is a development largely of the last two centuries. The founding of the United States of America provided a freer political environment for the Anglo-American than had been achieved by any previous government. England experienced the earliest industrial revolution of any European nation and had the most advanced technology up to the twentieth century. Throughout their history the United States and Canada have borrowed heavily from England's technology.

Spain, in contrast, declined economically after the sixteenth century and retained the essentials of its feudal system until the twentieth century. It was behind northern Europe in technology and industry even in the sixteenth century, and stayed behind as northern Europe advanced in the following centuries. The nineteenth-century revolutions in Latin America which gave rise to the independent nations we know today benefited largely the upper classes. The lower classes remained serfs on the land or workers in the mines or factories. As late as 1960 some of the Indians of Peru were forced to work three days per week for their landlords to pay their rent. This tax is higher than any imposed by the Inca nobles on the commoners of the early sixteenth century. The problem of raising the standard of living in Latin America is a difficult one because of the large Indian populations of illiterate and half-literate serfs held for centuries at the bottom of an outmoded feudal system. However, where an honest effort has been made, as in Mexico since the 1917 constitution, substantial progress has been achieved.

To sum up, it should be clear from this brief essay that the Spanish feudal system worked fairly well for the Spanish in the areas of advanced farming cultures in Mexico and Peru, where most of the Indians were accustomed to working at farming, at crafts, or on public works for an overlord. The same system failed among the intermediate farming cultures around the Caribbean and on the east coast of Brazil, because the Indian women farmed and the men there were not accustomed to being regimented as serfs on the land. In these areas the Spanish and Portuguese were soon forced to import slaves from west Africa, where slavery had occurred before the first Portuguese contact. The Spanish never obtained any significant cooperation from the hunting, gathering, and fishing Indians of southern Argentina and Chile, except from a few who became herders of cattle. They were even less successful among the nomadic and warlike Chichimecs of northeast Mexico. The Spanish colonies in New Mexico, where the Indian men were accustomed to working regularly at farming and crafts but never for an overlord, because their societies were democratic, exhibited an intermediate amount of cooperation between colonial boss and Indian worker.

The English in Anglo-America in the early stage of contact were reasonably successful in operating fur-trading posts, with the Indian men doing the actual hunting and trapping of the animals as they had done before White contact. But in the southern United States, where the plantation system for tobacco and cotton was introduced later, the Indian men were unsatisfactory workers because their women had done most of the farming before White contact; and they were soon replaced by African slaves. As immigrants from Europe increased on the east coast of the United States, the pressure for the Indian's land increased and continued unabated until the Pacific coast was reached.

In 1946 the Congress of the United States passed a law providing for a special court to hear complaints of Indian tribes over land claims. Since that time almost every tribe with any survivors at all has filed a claim against the U.S.A., and the majority of the more than one hundred cases heard in this court so far have been settled in favor of the Indians. We will eventually pay our Indians several billion dollars as compensation for the land we illegally took from them in the past, thus admitting that our land-grabbing methods have been unjust. The Indians are using most of this money to build schools, hospitals, roads, and irrigation projects on their reservations. This will help them to raise their standard of living and to attain their rightful place, economically and politically, as first-class citizens of the United States.

# THE CONTRIBUTIONS OF THE INDIANS
## TO MODERN LIFE

The dominant process of change in America since Columbus discovered it in A.D. 1492 has been the adaptation of the Indians to the ways of life introduced by Europeans. Some of this adjustment was voluntary on the part of the Indians, but most of it was forced upon them by the superior strength of the European conquerors; and even after new governments, such as the United States of America, were established in the New World, the dominance of a European-derived culture over that of the Indian continued, and is still continuing to this day. At the same time Indian cultures have had more influence on European cultures than most people are aware of. It is this backwash of acculturation of Whites to Indian ways of life that forms the subject of this chapter.

Probably all plants domesticated by the Indians are still eaten and are otherwise used somewhere in the Americas today, and many have been carried overseas to Europe, Asia, Africa, and the islands of the Pacific, where they furnish an important part of the diet at the present time. In Table I is assembled a list of the eight most heavily produced food crops for the year 1960, as given in the *Statistical Yearbook of the United Nations* for 1962. It is apparent from this list that production of the first four plants exceeds that of the last four and of all other food plants by a wide margin. Two of the first four, potatoes and maize, were first domesticated by Indians and were totally unknown or, in the case of maize, barely known in

Europe at the time Columbus discovered America. The combined production of potatoes and maize in 1960 slightly exceeds the combined production of wheat and rice, but the next four plants are all of Old World origin and thus throw the balance in favor of the Old World. However, at least one-third of the plant food in the world today is produced from plants first domesticated by Indians.

TABLE I

WORLD PRODUCTION IN METRIC TONS
OF STAPLE CROPS IN 1960

| | |
|---|---|
| Potatoes | 285,600,000 |
| Wheat | 244,100,000 |
| Rice | 239,300,000 |
| Maize | 214,300,000 |
| Barley | 93,200,000 |
| Oats | 54,100,000 |
| Rye | 37,200,000 |
| Soybeans | 27,300,000 |

The potato was widely raised by Indians in the Andean Highlands of South America in pre-Columbian times and was first brought to Europe by the Spaniards about 1570. From there it spread north and reached Ireland in 1606, where it became the most important food crop within the next fifty years. The term *Irish potato* was first used by an English herbalist in 1693, and the potato was first brought from Ireland to the United States in 1719 by a group of Irish Presbyterians.

Maize has continued to be an important article of diet in many parts of Latin America today, for instance, in Mexico, where about two-thirds of the total crop land is still planted in maize. In the United States we raise many times as much maize as Mexico, but most of it is fed to cattle and hogs. However, we consume a considerable quantity in the form of corn on the cob, cornbread, corn flakes, corn syrup, cornstarch, hominy, hominy grits, succotash (corn and Lima beans), and popcorn. Maize has achieved the rank of a staple food in parts of Asia and Africa.

If the American Indians had not domesticated any food plants,

the world today would have less to eat and population would be smaller. Because each plant grows best in a limited range of soils and climates, Old World domesticated plants would not flourish as well in the regions most suited to New World domesticates.

Turning to drugs and stimulants, tobacco is the best-known and most widely used nonedible American plant in the world today. It was first domesticated in South America, whence it spread north before A.D. 1492 to about the St. Lawrence River in North America, where the climate limited further northern dispersal. It was taken to Europe and raised there by about the midde of the sixteenth century, and thence was carried by European colonists to Africa, Oceania, Asia, and into Alaska from Siberia. Thus it spread around the world in about two centuries. New varieties of tobacco became established in many parts of the Old World and many, such as Turkish, are imported back into the New World today.

Native American alcoholic beverages are still consumed in large quantities in Latin America today; for instance, the consumption of pulque in Mexico exceeds that of all other alcoholic drinks combined. With the aid of distillation, introduced from Europe after the Spanish conquest, native drinks have been converted into hard liquors, such as the tequila and mescal of Mexico. Bourbon whiskey, a product of the United States, is made from the corn that the Indians were raising when the Whites arrived in the Americas.

Of the many native American drugs which have found their way into modern pharmacology, the best-known are coca in cocaine and novocaine, curare used in association with anesthetics, cinchona bark as the source of quinine, datura in pain-relievers, and cascara in laxatives. So impressed were the Spanish with Aztec medicine that they included courses in that subject in the curriculum of the College of Santa Cruz, established by the Franciscans in Mexico in 1536. Indian remedies continued to be widely used by Whites in the Americas until about one hundred years ago when scientific medicine began gradually to replace them. That Indian medicine was still going strong in the early twentieth century in the United States is illustrated by the sale of the Kickapoo Indian Medicine Company in 1911 for $250,000. This business had been operating for thirty years with as many as 150 medicine shows on the road at one time, all of them featuring one or more Kickapoo Indians.

One item of Indian furniture commonly used in the tropical forest of South America and around the Caribbean Sea has been widely adopted in Europe and the United States. This is the hammock. For centuries the hammock was the standard sleeping accommodation on ships of European cultures and their derivatives, in both their navies and merchant marines. It is still used by campers and by land travelers in the tropics. Before the discovery of America the hammock was unknown in the Old World.

The commercial cottons of the world today are derived principally from the species and varieties cultivated by American Indians before European contact. For instance, all the cotton raised today in the United States is of American Indian origin, as is the long-fiber cotton now raised in Egypt and other parts of Africa as well. The total world production of cotton in 1960 was about 11,000,000 metric tons, as compared to only 2,551,000 metric tons of wool. It is thus apparent that native American varieties of cotton supply much, if not most, of the world's clothing needs at the present time.

A few articles of Indian clothing have been widely adopted by European cultures and their derivatives. Most conspicuous of these is the parka, modeled on that of the Eskimo, but shorter and made of cotton, wool, or synthetic fibers instead of fur. From the Second World War until the present time the parka has been a standard article of issue for troops in cold climates. It is also a standard garment for sports costumes and children's wear. Another Indian item of current dress in the United States and Canada is the moccasin, and the moccasin toe has become increasingly popular in shoes made from leather tanned with tannic acid, a process of Old World origin. The poncho, of South American Indian origin, was issued to United States troops in the First World War, and has continued to be used as a raincoat by various peoples around the world. Ponchos of rubberized materials or plastic are now spreading from the United States back into Latin American countries, where they are eagerly sought by those who can afford them.

It was from the Indians that Europeans first learned to make rubber, a substance indispensable to twentieth-century technological development. Indians from Brazil to Mexico used the sap from native trees to make a variety of objects ranging from enema syringes to rubber balls used in athletic and ceremonial games.

The greatest works of American Indian art ceased to be produced or were deliberately destroyed by the Spanish conquerors as soon as they gained political control of the New World. This art, from Mexico to Bolivia, had been closely associated with the nobility and the priesthood and, in conquering the Indian nobility and stamping out the heathen religions, the Spanish eradicated the art as well as the human sacrifice and other shocking aspects of Indian religions. The best examples of American Indian architecture were torn down and the stone was used to build Christian churches. After this almost complete obliteration of American Indian art and architecture, the world was forced to wait until archeology rediscovered these distinctive art styles in order to become fully aware of their existence. It is largely for this reason that American Indian art has only recently been granted a place among the great art styles of the world.

In the territory that is now the United States, Indians early became the subjects of paintings; for instance, Gustavus Hesselius painted a series of masterly portraits of Lenape chiefs as early as 1735. When a number of Indian chiefs visited Washington, D.C. in the 1820's, they posed for portraits which became the nucleus of the famous "Indian Gallery." As many as 120 of these portraits were published from 1836-1844 in a three-volume folio edition entitled *History of the Indian Tribes of North America* by McKenny and Hall. A number of artists went west of the Mississippi and painted Indians in their home environment. The most famous of this group was George Catlin, who exhibited his paintings of Indian life in Eastern cities in the late 1830's and gave lectures and pantomimes about Indians.

Art produced by Indians of the twentieth century is experiencing a period of renascence in many parts of the Americas. In the southwestern United States, for instance, weaving, pottery-making, silversmithing and painting have shown an increase both in quantity and quality. This is due in part to an expanding market for these products and also to increased emphasis on the teaching of art to Indian children in the schools.

Mexico, more than any other contemporary American nation, has developed since its 1917 revolution a national art style which is an integration of Spanish and Indian elements. At the hands of such masters as Diego Rivera, José Clemente Orozco, David Alfaro Siqueiros, Rufino Tamayo, Miguel Covarrubias, and Juan O'Gorman, this art style came to life and may be seen today in Mexico in such public places as the *Palacio de Belles Artes*, the *Palacio Nacional*, and the National University of Mexico.

The earliest recorded attempt in the United States to utilize Indian themes in music composed for mass consumption was that of James Hewitt in 1794, who used Cherokee themes in a musical play about Indians called *Tammany*. One of the songs entitled "Alk'amoonok, the Death Song of the Cherokee Indians" was published as sheet music in 1799 and became very popular. Music said to be based on Indian themes was composed and published for popular consumption throughout most of the nineteenth century, but it was not until Edward MacDowell composed his *Indian Suite* in 1891-92 that authentic Indian music was used by an American composer. MacDowell drew from a published collection of Indian songs obtained by Theodore Baker on the Seneca reservation and at the Carlisle Indian School in the summer of 1880. In 1893 Alice Fletcher published a monograph on Omaha Indian songs and two of her songs, together with three others, have since been incorporated in "Indian Lore," a pamphlet in the Merit Badge Series of the Boy Scouts of America. About 100,000 copies of this pamphlet have been printed to date and tens of thousands of Boy Scouts have learned three songs, including the Omaha tribal prayer, to acquire the merit badge. Although musical plays and more serious operas making some use of Indian musical materials were composed in the first thirty years of the twentieth century in the United States, none of them have survived in the operatic repertoire of today. They achieved popular success for only a few decades.

In Latin America the early compositions of Carlos Chavez in Mexico and of Heitor Villa-Lobos in Brazil made use of Indian themes and achieved a moderate success with them, but neither composer has used Indian materials in recent years. On the whole, therefore, Indian music has had little influence on musical composition of the present day, and much less influence than African music on current popular jazz and jive.

The European languages now dominating speech in the Americas, namely, Spanish, Portuguese, English, and French, have all been influenced by Indian languages. Perhaps as many as fifty thousand Indian words have been incorporated into these languages. For instance, twenty-three of the states in the United States have Indian names. Examples of Indian words incorporated into English are tobacco, hominy, succotash, toboggan, moccasin, wampum, wigwam, tipi, squaw, and papoose. Buck (for dollar) harks back to the fur trade days when a buckskin was a unit of value. A number of phrases, such as *Indian summer, Indian giver, go on the warpath, bury the hatchet, run the gauntlet,* and *war paint* for women's make-up are meaningful only in light of Indian culture.

With respect to literature, that of the United States often centers around the Indians. In the novels of James Fenimore Cooper, written from 1823 to 1851, his hero, Leatherstocking, was the first non-Indian man in fiction to become acculturated to Indian customs, language, and values, and to prefer many of them to those of his own culture. He was a sort of superman who was reverent about religion, fearless of danger, and fair and just in his dealings with both Indians and Whites. Cooper's *The Last of the Mohicans* has been rated as the best-known American novel in Europe and the rest of the literate world. Cooper never lived with Indians but derived most of his information about them from the writings of a Moravian missionary among the Delaware Indians, J. G. E. Heckwelder.

Henry Wadsworth Longfellow's *Hiawatha* was published in 1855 and had sold fifty thousand copies by five months after publication. This highly romantic poem was based on H. R. Schoolcraft's *Algic Researches* (1839) on the Ojibwa Indians, with whom Schoolcraft had lived and from whom he had taken a wife.

In the famous dime-novel series that first became popular in the 1860's, Indians played roles in 45 per cent of the 321 stories.

Indians continued to be popular with literary authors in the twentieth century. They figured prominently in the poems and plays of Mary Austin. Among the novels, Oliver LaFarge's *Laughing Boy* (1939) achieved great success. One literary critic lists thirty-seven novels or collections of short stories on Indians for the first half of the twentieth century. This figure is exceeded by only one other minority group in the United States, the Negro.

The twentieth century has also witnessed a great many Indian plays or stories in motion pictures, radio, and television. Some of the early Indian movies are *Hiawatha* (1909), *Deerslayer* (1911), and *The Last of the Mohicans* (1920). The last decade or two has witnessed a change in the character of the Indians portrayed from that of an incorrigibly evil personality to an originally noble soul whose acts of violence, if any, are caused directly from bad treatment at the hands of other peoples. In short, the noble savage has returned.

On a more serious level, the psychoanalyst Carl Jung stated in 1928 that he could observe an Indian component in the character of some of his American patients.

Indian history and lore has also contributed to a number of modern religions in the Americas. The Roman Catholicism of much of Latin America is a blend of Christian and Indian beliefs and practices. Although the names of native gods have been eliminated by the Catholic clergy, the Indians assign the attributes of these gods to the Virgin Mary and the Saints and expect the images of the Catholic pantheon to cure disease, control the weather, and keep them from harm, much as they thought their pagan gods did.

The Mexican Indians have their own Virgin, called the Virgin of Guadalupe. According to one version of the legend, a newly baptized Indian named Juan Diego was tapping the juice of maguey plants on a hill north of Mexico City in 1531, when a dark-complexioned Indian virgin appeared before him and told him that she wished a church to be built in her honor on the very spot where she was standing. Diego finally gained the audience of Bishop Zumarraga, but the Bishop would not believe his story. When the virgin contacted the Indian a second time, she directed him to a beautiful garden of roses growing miraculously among the cacti, and he wrapped some of the roses in his cloak and went again to the bishop. But when he opened the cloak, lo and behold, it contained not roses but a painting of the Virgin. The bishop then accepted the Indian's experience as a miracle and passed knowledge of it on to the Pope, who stated that no other race in history had been honored in such a manner. A church was then built at the foot of the hill, in the town of Guadalupe, the picture was placed in it, and it thus became the most sacred shrine for all the Indians of Mexico.

Several minor religions in the United States have also been influenced by Indian cultures. One such religion is the United Society of Believers, popularly known as Shakers (not to be confused with a predominantly Indian cult of that name in Washington and Oregon). The saintliness of the founder of the Shaker religion, Mother Ann, was established on the basis of the testimony of Indians who saw a bright light around her on one occasion and proclaimed her goodness on another when they met her returning from her eastern mission at the Albany (New York) ferry. Indian spirits are thought to have imparted songs to the Shakers and to have turned up in large numbers at one of their services, where they possessed the bodies of a dozen Shakers, who yelled and cavorted like Indians and demanded succotash to eat.

The largest and most restrained modern religion in the United States that shows Indian influence is the Church of Jesus Christ of Latter-day Saints. *The Book of Mormon,* published in 1830, is probably derived from an unpublished manuscript written by Solomon Spaulding, in which he postulates that the Indians who built the many mounds in Ohio were descendants of the Lamanites, a rebellious tribe of Jews. Abandoned by God, these renegade Jews of the first millennium B.C. are said to have wandered to the Americas, losing much of their civilization along the way. The Mormons accept this view of the origin of the Indians. And what is more striking, they believe that the second coming of Christ actually occurred in Mexico, where he is said to have appeared before three thousand Indians on one occasion, a greater number on the next day, and to have made several later appearances among them. The myths of the White Gods among the Aztecs, Mayas, Toltecs, and Incas are interpreted by the Mormons as further evidence for the appearance of Christ in the Americas.

It is apparent from this brief essay that the Indians exerted a significant influence on the cultures of the Europeans who first conquered them, settled amongst them, and finally gave them citizenship in the new nations created in the New World.

## References

Harold E. Driver, Indians of North America (Chicago: The University of Chicago Press, 1961), Chap. 26.

A. Irving Hallowell, "The Backwash of the Frontier: the Impact of the Indian on American Culture," *Smithsonian Report for 1958* (1959), pp. 447-72.

# FURTHER READINGS

Astrov, Margot, *The Winged Serpent: an Anthology of American Indian Prose and Poetry*. New York: The John Day Co., Inc., 1946. An excellent collection of Indian literature from the Arctic to Peru.

Baudin, Louis, *Daily Life in Peru under the last Incas*. Translated from the French by Winifred Bradford. London: George Allen & Unwin, 1961. A good description of the Incas on the eve of Spanish discovery.

————, *A Socialist Empire; the Incas of Peru*. Translated from the French by Katherine Woods; ed. Arthur Goddard. Princeton, N.J.: D. Van Nostrand Co., Inc., 1961. More scholarly than the work above, but well written.

Beals, Carleton, *Nomads and Empire Builders; Native Peoples and Cultures of South America*. Philadelphia: Chilton Co., 1961. The best treatment of the subject at general reader level.

Bennett, Wendell C., *Ancient Arts of the Andes*. New York: The Museum of Modern Art, 1954. A fine selection of art objects figured in 203 halftones and 5 color plates.

Bingham, Hiram, *Lost City of the Incas*. New York: Atheneum Publishers, 1963. Describes the discovery, excavation, and history of Machu Picchu, the famous mountain city of the Incas.

Birket-Smith, Kaj, *The Eskimos*. London: Methuen & Co., Ltd., 1959. The best general book on the Eskimos.

Caso, Alfonso, *The Aztecs: People of the Sun*. Illustrated by Miguel Covarrubias; translated by Lowell Dunham. Norman: University of Oklahoma Press, 1958. The best book on Aztec religion, with 42 drawings in as many as six colors, and 16 halftones.

Catlin, George, *Episodes from Life Among the Indians and Last Rambles.* Norman: University of Oklahoma Press, 1959. Covers South American Indians and North American Indians west of the Rocky Mountains. Includes 152 scenes and portraits by the author done from 1830 to 1855.

Collier, John, *Indians of the Americas.* New York: The New American Library, 1947. A compact overview of the Indians of the two continents with emphasis on their welfare under White domination.

Covarrubias, Miguel, *The Eagle, the Jaguar, and the Serpent; Indian Art of the Americas.* New York: Alfred A. Knopf, Inc., 1954. Among the best treatments of the subject for North America. Many original drawings, some in color, by the author, a distinguished Mexican artist.

————, *Indian Art of Mexico and Central America.* New York: Alfred A. Knopf, Inc., 1957. Another fine volume on the art of its area with illustrations by the author.

Day, A. Grove, *The Sky Clears: Poetry of the American Indians.* New York: The Macmillan Company, 1951. An excellent collection of the poetry of North American Indians, including the Aztecs and Mayas of Mexico.

Dockstader, Frederick J., *Indian Art in America; the Arts and Crafts of the North American Indian.* Greenwich, Conn.: New York Graphic Society, 1961. Outstanding both in the selection of art objects and in their reproduction.

Driver, Harold E., *Indians of North America.* Chicago: The University of Chicago Press, 1961. The leading comparative general work on Indians from the Arctic to Panama.

Drucker, Philip, *Indians of the Northwest Coast.* Garden City, N.Y.: The Natural History Press, 1963. The best introduction to this area.

Durán, Fray Diego, *The Aztecs: the History of the Indies of New Spain,* edited, translated, and annotated by Doris Heyden and Fernando Horcasitas. New York: The Orion Press, 1963. The first English translation of this sixteenth-century work by a Spanish priest and historian.

Ewers, John C., *The Blackfeet: Raiders on the Northwestern Plains.* Norman: University of Oklahoma Press, 1958. A fine account of its history and civilization by the leading authority on this tribe.

Freyre, Gilberto, *The Masters and the Slaves* (2nd ed.). New York: Alfred A. Knopf, Inc., 1956. Of this classic work by the dean of Brazilian ethnologists, almost a third is devoted to Indians.

Hagan, William T., *American Indians.* Chicago: The University of Chicago Press, 1961. The best short history of Indian and White relations in the United States.

d'Harcourt, Raoul, *Textiles of Ancient Peru and their techniques.* Edited by Grace G. Denny and Carolyn M. Osborne; translated by Sadie Brown. Seattle: University of Washington Press, 1962. A classic work on weaving, for which the Incas were famous.

Inverarity, Robert Bruce, *Art of the Northwest Coast Indians.* Berkeley: University of California Press, 1950. The best book on the art of this area.

Jennings, Jesse D., and Edward Norbeck, eds., *Prehistoric Man in the New World.* Chicago: The University of Chicago Press, 1963. A volume of essays by experts in this field.

Kelemen, Pál, *Medieval American Art* (2nd ed.). New York: The Macmillan Company, 1956. Unsurpassed on the art of Mexico and Peru.

Kroeber, Theodora, *The Inland Whale.* Bloomington: Indiana University Press, 1959. Nine tales of California Indians, with women as central characters, told in a most readable style.

———, *Ishi in Two Worlds.* Berkeley and Los Angeles: University of California Press, 1961. A sensitive biography of the last "wild" California Indian, who lived fifty years in the Stone Age in the northern part of the state and five in San Francisco from 1911 to 1916.

Lothrop, Samuel K., *Pre-Columbian Art.* New York: Phaidon Press (distributed by Garden City Books), 1957. Another fine book on the Indian art of Latin America.

Lowie, Robert H., *The Crow Indians.* New York: Holt, Rinehart & Winston, Inc., 1956. The most readable book on this well-known Plains tribe, by the leading authority on their way of life.

———, *Indians of the Plains.* Garden City, N.Y.: The Natural History Press, 1963. The best introduction to this area.

Mason, John Alden, *The Ancient Civilizations of Peru.* Middlesex: Harmondsworth (Penguin Books), 1957. One of the best books on these complex civilizations.

Mead, Margaret, and Ruth L. Bunzel, *The Golden Age of American Anthropology.* New York: George Braziller, 1960. A large book of readings on North American Indians from 1519 to 1920. Begins with a good selection of readable early material but becomes progressively more technical after writings by anthropologists are introduced.

Morley, Sylvanus G., *The Ancient Maya.* Stanford: Stanford University Press, 1946. A classic on this famous people.

Powell, Philip Wayne, *Soldiers, Indians, and Silver.* Berkeley and Los Angeles: University of California Press, 1952. The story of the Spanish-Indian struggle on the silver frontier of 16th century Mexico.

Prescott, William Hickling, *Histories: the Rise and Decline of the Spanish Empire.* New York: The Viking Press, Inc., 1963. Selections from four of Prescott's books, including *The Conquest of Mexico* and *The Conquest of Peru,* which give considerable space to the Aztecs and Incas.

Soustelle, Jacques, *The Daily Life of the Aztecs on the Eve of the Spanish Conquest.* Translated from the French by Patrick O'Brian. New York: The Macmillan, Company, 1962. The best book on the everyday life of this famous people.

Spicer, Edward H., *Cycles of Conquest: The Impact of Spain, Mexico & the U.S. on Indians of the Southwest, 1533-1960.* Tucson: University of Arizona Press, 1960. A large scholarly work, but eminently readable.

Stewart, Julian H., and Louis C. Faron, *Native Peoples of South America.* New York: McGraw-Hill, Inc., 1959. The leading text in its field.

Thompson, John Eric Sidney, *Maya Hieroglyphic Writing; an Introduction.* Norman: University of Oklahoma Press, 1960. Technical, but well-written.

———, *The Rise and Fall of Maya Civilization.* Norman: University of Oklahoma Press, 1954. Contains excellent sections on the personality, philosophy, art, and intellectual achievement of this most sophisticated Indian civilization.

Underhill, Ruth Murray, *The Navajos.* Norman: University of Oklahoma Press, 1958. The best single volume on the largest tribe in the United States.

———, *Red Man's America.* Chicago: The University of Chicago Press, 1953. A good introduction to the Indians of the United States.

Vaillant, George C., *Aztecs of Mexico.* Garden City, N.Y.: Doubleday & Company, Inc., 1941. The most widely read book in English on the Aztecs. Later editions in paperback. Recently revised by the author's wife.

Von Hagen, Victor Wolfgang, *The Ancient Sun Kingdoms of the Americas.* Cleveland: The World Publishing Company, 1961. A good summary of these complex civilizations.

———, *The Aztec: Man and Tribe.* New York: The New American Library, 1958. A compact summary, comparable to that of Vaillant.

———, *The Incas; People of the Sun.* Cleveland: The World Publishing Company, 1961. A brief but useful description of this famous people.

———, *World of the Maya.* New York: The New American Library, 1960. A good short account of this remarkable people.

Wauchope, Robert, *Lost Tribes and Sunken Continents.* Chicago: University of Chicago Press, 1962. Discusses and evaluates a grand slam of both "crackpot" and scientifically demonstrable views on the origin of the American Indians.

Weatherwax, Paul, *Indian Corn in Old America*. New York: The Macmillan Company, 1954. A nontechnical work by a botanist on the history and geography of corn on both continents; sixty-six pages of line drawings and halftones, three illustrations in color.

Wissler, Clark, *The American Indian* (3rd ed.). New York: Oxford University Press, Inc., 1938. The leading comparative work on the two continents for its time; reprinted since 1938 by Peter Smith, Publisher, New York.

Wolf, Eric R., *Sons of the Shaking Earth*. Chicago: University of Chicago Press, 1959. A comprehensive view of the Indians of Mexico and Guatemala from prehistoric times to the mid-twentieth century.

# THE GLOBAL HISTORY SERIES